Write.

10 Days to
Overcome
Writer's Block.
Period.

Karen E. Peterson, Ph.D.

Adams Media
Avon, Massachusetts

Published by Adams Media, an F+W Publications Company
57 Littlefield Street
Avon, MA 02322
www.adamsmedia.com

ISBN: 1-59337-503-4
Printed in Canada.
J I H G F E D C B A

Library of Congress Cataloging-in-Publication Data
Peterson, Karen E.
Write : 10 days to overcome writer's block : period / by Karen E. Peterson.
p. cm.
Includes bibliographical references and index.
ISBN 1-59337-503-4
1. Writer's block. 2. Authorship--Psychological aspects. I. Title: 10 days to
overcome writer's block. II. Title.

PN171.W74P48 2006
808'.02019--dc22

2005033325

This publication is designed to provide accurate and authoritative information
with regard to the subject matter covered. It is sold with the understanding
that the publisher is not engaged in rendering legal, accounting, or other
professional advice. If legal advice or other expert assistance is required, the
services of a competent professional person should be sought.

—From a *Declaration of Principles* jointly adopted by a Committee of the
American Bar Association and a Committee of Publishers and Associations

Many of the designations used by manufacturers and sellers to distinguish their
product are claimed as trademarks. Where those designations appear in this
book and Adams Media was aware of a trademark claim, the designations have
been printed with initial capital letters.

This book is available at quantity discounts for bulk purchases.
For information, please call 1-800-872-5627.

Dedication

For Kurt Vonnegut,
Who keeps us laughing
all the way to the gallows
and back.

. . . and for Denise Levertov,
who so elegantly
granted me
permission
to write.

. . . and for Steven A. Carreras,
who has helped me
see clearly
now.

Is there something that will go unsaid if you don't write?
—Denise Levertov, personal communication, 1987

The plot is just a bribe to keep them reading.
—Kurt Vonnegut, Case Western Reserve University, 1985

contents

appendices:
your "to-go" order of motivation

Acknowledgments

There are so many people who have helped in the creation of this book, I could probably write another book about how grateful I am for their support. I am especially appreciative of the work done by so many clinicians and researchers who have pioneered the area of writing as therapy (in particular, Dr. Lucia Capacchione and Dr. James Pennebaker), as well as those who have helped us to understand the different functions of the left and right sides of the brain (most notably, Dr. R. Joseph and Dr. Allan Schore).

I'd also like to thank my agent, Linda Roghaar, for her wisdom, unswerving support, and marvelous sense of humor. I'd like to thank my editor, Paula Munier, as well as Andrea Norville, Jason Flynn, and the rest of the staff at Adams Media for their tireless support, attention to detail, and belief in my work.

I would also like to thank Christine Belleris for her perennial support of my ideas. I thank Lisa Ellis for being my friend/editor/kindred spirit—and especially for her encouragement in the creation of this book and my first two novels. I thank Paula Morgan-Johnson, who helped this book come to fruition and who encouraged me to use my voice. And, just because, I want to thank Abby Nelson for her concentric circles of effervescent support, wit, and artistic inspiration.

A special and timeless thank-you goes out to Steven A. Carreras, who has helped me see clearly now.

I also thank Kurt Vonnegut for his written snippets of support and encouragement over the years and for his fiction, which has so strongly influenced my own sense of gallows humor and the absurd. And, finally, I thank Denise Levertov, for unwittingly giving me permission to write one warm spring afternoon.

Author's Note

And why do I know so much about writer's block? Because I've had it—in both senses of this phrase.

I've also "had it" across genres (fiction, nonfiction, poetry), and across careers (English teacher, psychologist, and workshop facilitator).

Now, it's not that I never get blocked—I just know what to do about it. Finally.

Over the past twenty years, with clients as well as program participants, I've developed the *bi-vocal approach* to conquering writer's block. It's really this simple: We need to fight writer's block with both sides of the brain, but most of us use only one side. As Dr. R. Joseph says in his groundbreaking book, *The Right Brain and the Unconscious: Discovering the Stranger Within*:

> Although the right brain appears to be the more creative aspect of the mind, for example, in the form of artistic expression, creativity is possibly a product of having two brains and two minds. Indeed, the creative process is perhaps made possible, at least in part, by the interpretation and guesswork that occur when the two different brains and regions of the mind tackle the same problem and then try to communicate with each other. (pp. 201–202)

Along with the work of Dr. Joseph, I would like to express my appreciation for the work of so many other researchers and clinicians who—unbeknownst to them—contributed to the origins of the bi-vocal approach, which has a strong foundation in research and clinical practice. For example, psychologists such as Dr. James Pennebaker (*Opening Up* and *Writing to Heal*) have conducted extensive research on the therapeutic effects of writing about stress, and the American Psychological Association has recently published a book comprised of research articles on the therapeutic power of writing (*The Writing Cure*). These research results have provided the basis for the bi-vocal approach's use of writing as a form of stress management and self-knowledge.

Additionally, over the last few decades, some clinicians began to use writing to access the right side of the brain (albeit *without* asking the *same* questions of the left side of the brain). For example, as a form of what Gestalt therapists call "dialoguing," in an attempt to access the "disowned parts of the self," some practitioners asked clients to write with their nondominant hand, and this approach was then popularized in self-help books by therapists such as Dr. Lucia Capacchione (*The Power of Your Other Hand*) and John Bradshaw (*Homecoming*). Additionally, Dr. Capacchione also encouraged readers to write back and forth with both hands; however, she has focused primarily on issues such as childhood trauma rather than writer's block, and she has erroneously assumed that the nondominant hand will by definition express the voice of an encouraging, creative self. Nevertheless, I am thankful for her groundbreaking work in this area, which helped provide the impetus for my work with writers.

Other researchers and therapists have focused on alternately stimulating the right and left sides of the brain, although they have not specifically used writing as a modality. For example, Dr. Fredric Schiffer (*Of Two Minds*) has conducted research and provided treatment through what he calls "dual brain psychology," in which he asks clients to cover one eye while thinking about a problem for a few minutes, then switch and cover the other eye while thinking about the same problem—often with strikingly different results, as displayed in simultaneous brain scans. Similarly, positive research results have also been reported by practitioners of EMDR (see *Eye Movement Desensitization and Reprocessing* by Francine Shapiro), who employ *bilateral stimulation of the brain*—providing rapidly alternating sensory stimulation (through lights, sounds, or tactile pulsars) to the right and left brain hemispheres—in order to help clients in psychotherapy change. These clinicians and researchers have provided the basis for the bi-vocal approach's use of activating the "voices" of both sides of the brain.

In building upon—and with much appreciation of—the earlier work of these researchers and practitioners, I have designed the bi-vocal approach as a specific technique for overcoming writer's block. The two main components of the bi-vocal approach are the *parallel monologue* (in which, for comparative purposes, each side of the brain answers the same question or responds to the same checklist) and the *interior dialogue* (in which the two sides of the brain "converse" by responding to questions that are specifically designed to help writers).

The bi-vocal approach may be used for self-help or in conjunction with psychotherapy conducted by a licensed mental health professional. *However, please note that the bi-vocal approach is not intended as a substitute for psychotherapy.*

shaping your life as a writer

the bi-vocal way

CHAPTER 1

permission to write:

how to find both your voices (and ditch theirs)

Wake up!
For God's sake, wake up, wake up!
Free will, free will!

—Kurt Vonnegut

I have heard mothers tell of the long night with their firstborn when they were afraid that they and the baby might die. And I have heard my grandmother speak of her first ball when she was seventeen. And they were all, when their souls grew warm, poets.

—Ray Bradbury

Picture this:

You, with a Big Block of time; a serene, aesthetically pleasing hotel suite with free daily massages, a pool, and a delightful café; a privacy agreement signed by encouraging family members, friends, and coworkers (though you may of course call them); breakfast in bed from room service with abundant choices from bacon and espresso to granola and green tea; pads of paper and a box of pens in your favorite colors; and an absolutely perfect laptop.

Sound about right?

"Oh, yes," says the right side of your brain. "Nothing less will do."

"Not going to happen," says the left side of your brain. "So just write!"

While these two voices bicker away, the wraith of writer's block arises like gossamer smoke to swath your Muse in such a fog that the possibility of writing—albeit your first love—truly becomes Mission Impossible.

For example, let's take the case of Robert, a newly minted accountant who had just taken over the family business—even though he yearned to be a writer. His main complaint was that he never had time to write. He was too busy managing accounts, checking e-mails, attending to his family, and worrying about finances to sit down and write the Great Un-American Novel. Although scenes from his novel had flashed through his mind for years, he either didn't take the time to jot them down, or, even if he did jot them on slips of paper, the backs of magazines, or restaurant napkins, he'd lose track of these snippets of creativity scattered throughout his car, home, office, pockets, and briefcase. He never had time to organize these jigsaw pieces, and he wasn't sure about the plot. He didn't know where or how to start, so . . . he just *didn't*.

Sound familiar?

Of course, my first suggestion for Robert was that he honor his creative work by giving it a home. I asked him to go to his favorite office supply store and purchase a portable receptacle for his bursts of creativity: a clear vinyl pouch, a plastic pocket folder, a vinyl index card holder (with blank index cards), even a pencil case—anything he could carry with him at all times. I have offered this suggestion to many others over the years, just as I am offering it to you now: Buy a container for your Muse's musings, as a first step in learning to respect your work as a writer.

This is just one of many approaches I've used to help writers claim their right to write. I have written this book because, as a writer of fiction and nonfiction, I, too, have struggled with writer's block, forever craving that Big Block of time that never seemed to materialize. As a psychologist, I've spent twenty years helping writers search for the Muse who's gone AWOL once again, and as a university writing instructor, I've watched while my students frantically tried to find their voices.

All too often, the writer's world is viewed as mysterious—and reserved for the chosen few: the blockbuster novelist, the literary elite, the slammer journalist. The rest of us feel like impostors. But the world of writing is open to anyone, anytime, anyplace.

You are one of those anyones.

And so am I. This I discovered when I first met poet Denise Levertov. I had already overheard Kurt Vonnegut say, when pressed for a formula for his convoluted plot lines, that "the plot is just a bribe to keep them reading." Could I come up with a decent bribe? Probably—I have all the books on plot that are still in print. I certainly knew I had a lot to say, and I even knew I had some talent for writing, but I still couldn't answer—let alone ask—the quintessential writer's question.

But that day, not long after I had defected from teaching college English to attend a doctoral program in psychology, I crawled out from my ten-year volcanic pit of writer's block, planted one foot on solid ground, and posed to Ms. Levertov the unnerving question that had haunted me for years.

"What," I asked with some trepidation, "gives one the right to write?"

She knew exactly what I meant. Without skipping a beat, she said, "Well, is there something that will go unsaid if you *don't* write?"

"Of course," I said.

"Well, then, you simply must write," she said. "It's like breathing."

Accompanied by the echo of her footsteps as she walked up the stairs and I sauntered down, I realized she had somehow given me permission to write—which is exactly what happens every time I tell this story to a budding writer. Although it takes a certain amount of ego to be a writer in the first place, many of us have a hard time claiming this right to write. It's as if behind all those brilliant ideas scribbled on countless scraps of paper, there lurks an impostor within.

The majority of writers who consult with me say, "I just don't know where to begin." What they really mean is: "I don't know *how to dare* to begin." They have stacks of unread books on writing novels, creativity, and becoming a freelance writer. But even if they dare to read these books, they are still thwarted by a voice that says, *"Who am I to think I can write? Sooner or later, they'll all find out I'm just an impostor."*

This impostor within resides in the right side of the brain—about two doors down from the Muse. Most books on writing focus on left-brain "just-do-it" methods or right-brain creativity exercises, but the impostor within may still resist all attempts at self-expression. What makes this book different? *You will learn how to conquer this impostor within by using new methods derived from the findings of recent brain research.*

Brain research? Sounds fishy to me, too. But the reality is that there's plenty of room for both art and science when it comes to the creative process. Imagine my surprise when I woke up one day and realized I've got one foot in each world. I'm a psychologist and a novelist, a shrink and a poet, a therapist and an essayist—you name it, I'll either analyze it or write about it, or both. And that is precisely my point.

As writers, most of us are terrified that seeing a shrink will kill the Muse. We are convinced that our art grows out of our suffering, and if we let some Freudians take away the suffering, then they'll take away our writing voices, too. Perhaps this is true for a few writers, but in my twenty-seven years of experience with writers—seven as English teacher, twenty as shrink—the opposite has been true.

Usually, when writers consult with me, it's because their art is *not* growing out of their suffering. They're just suffering: feelings of inadequacy, a second divorce, one last chance at tenure, brilliant ideas but no follow-through, fear of the editor's red pen, stagnating in a dead-end job with no time to write, stuck in the too-many-letters-of-rejection rut, lost in the plot-isn't-going-anywhere quagmire, riddled with publication anxiety—you name it, but none of it adds up to the notion of sculpting art out of suffering. Not even an ashtray out of this.

That's why I wrote this book: If we have suffered—and who among us hasn't—and we can summon the will to write, then the next step may be to write about that suffering. It doesn't necessarily mean that we'll *publish* what we say about our angst, but it may be necessary to write about it before we can publish what we want to put out there.

In other words, write for yourself. In the days of James Joyce, writers wrote in order to say something—not to hit the bestseller list. In the days of Shakespeare, writers wrote to express their hopes and dreams about the universal themes of humanity—not to get on Oprah's book list. As W. H. Auden so aptly states:

> Someone says, "Whom do you write for?"
> I reply: "Do you read me?"
> If they say, "Yes," I say, "Do you like it?"
> If they say, "No," then I say, "I don't write for you."

Sounds good to me—but tell that to any writer who wants those fifteen minutes of fame in *Publishers Weekly*. In today's world, the focus appears to be on what happens *after* we write: Send out those queries, get an agent, get a publisher, get media exposure—get your work out there! Sadly, these are the realities of today's publishing arena. But if these are the main focus *while we're trying to write*, they're likely to ignite what Ray Bradbury calls those "live mines" in our brains.

To illustrate, let me offer you one of my favorite top ten lists—I call it the Top Ten Reasons to Avoid Writing. Check off any statements that resonate with you, and feel free to fill in the blanks at the end.

Top Ten Reasons to Avoid Writing

_10. I might not get published.
__ 9. I might get published.
__ 8. Nobody will read my book.
__ 7. Somebody will read my book.
__ 6. It won't make the bestseller list.
__ 5. It will make the bestseller list.
__ 4. The critics will hate it.
__ 3. The critics will love it.
__ 2. If I'm a bestselling author, I'll have to give up____.
__ 1. If I'm a bestselling author, I'll have to accept____.

As you can see, it's easy to have some ambivalence about how our work will be received by the world. If you want to see what ambivalence really looks like, do this next exercise below.

Try to respond to this list again, but this time check off your responses and fill in the blanks by writing with your other (nondominant) hand. Don't just copy your previous answers. Instead, switch to the other hand, let your pen linger there for a moment, close your eyes, then open them, and see what pops out. You'll probably have to print in block letters, but this is no time to worry about handwriting. Just see what happens.

Top Ten Reasons to Avoid Writing

_10. I might not get published.

_ 9. I might get published.

_ 8. Nobody will read my book.

_ 7. Somebody will read my book.

_ 6. It won't make the bestseller list.

_ 5. It will make the bestseller list.

_ 4. The critics will hate it.

_ 3. The critics will love it.

_ 2. If I'm a bestselling author, I'll have to give up____.

_ 1. If I'm a bestselling author, I'll have to accept____.

Now, that's what I call ambivalence. When I responded to this two-part exercise, which I call *parallel monologue*, I could tell that one hand clearly did not know what the other was doing. For example, my dominant hand checked off number 10 (I might not get published) and number 7 (Somebody will read my book). Then, my dominant hand wrote (in number 2) that I'd have to give up "my practice," and (in number 1) that I'd have to accept "I'm a good writer."

On the other hand—pun intended—my nondominant hand checked off number 9 (I might get published), number 7 (Somebody will read my book), number 6 (It won't make the bestseller list), and number 5 (It will make the bestseller list). My nondominant hand then added (in number 2) that I'd have to give up "being a victim," and (in number 1) that I'd have to accept "all the time I wasted." Talk about conflict! It's amazing I'm even bothering to finish this chapter.

Most people get different responses when they switch hands—because they are accessing the other side of the brain. If you notice that your answers are exactly the same, and I mean exactly, then try both exercises again when no one else is around. Sometimes the presence or possible intrusion of others can be inhibiting.

Left Brain Versus Right Brain

So what's all this have to do with brain research? Researchers such as Dr. R. Joseph have documented that the right side of the brain controls the left side of the body, and vice versa. The majority of people (85 percent) are right-handed, and are therefore left-brain dominant. However, even left-handed individuals (who are split fifty-fifty between being truly right-brain dominant versus of mixed brain dominance) must contend with the two radically different sides of the brain—which tend to disagree about when, where, and how we should write.

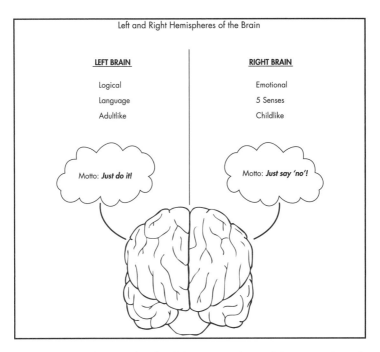

Left and Right Hemispheres of the Brain

LEFT BRAIN

Logical

Language

Adultlike

Motto: *Just do it!*

RIGHT BRAIN

Emotional

5 Senses

Childlike

Motto: *Just say 'no'!*

The "just-do-it" left side of the brain is logical, language-based, and adultlike. On the other hand, the "just-say-no" right side of the brain is dominant for emotion, negative memories, and sensory input (e.g., visual stimulation). This means that, even though the logical left brain may exhort us to write, the right brain remembers every hypercritical voice we've ever heard, and is more than happy to replay them, en masse, every time we try to write.

And, just to make sure we get really blocked, the right brain, being more in tune with emotion, is also more closely connected to the command center for the classic fight-or-flight anxiety response, which can be triggered automatically by the sight of a desk filled with unfinished writing projects—or no projects at all. According to Dr. Joseph, although both sides of the brain are connected to the limbic system—our brain's most primitive and reactive emotional center—the right side of the brain, being dominant for the recognition and expression of emotion, is more likely to pick up the fight-or-flight signal. Meanwhile, researcher Dr. Allan Schore has also pointed out that the right brain is dominant for the release of our favorite stress hormone, cortisol, which makes us sometimes just too edgy to write.

Not only are the two sides of the brain at odds with each other in terms of their different functions—they also don't get along very well. This is because the gnarly cord that connects the two sides of the brain, the corpus callosum, serves more as a barrier than a bridge. However, if we want to activate our writing selves, we need to tap into both sides of the brain. In using what I call the *bi-vocal approach*, we can listen to the voices of both sides of the brain—and it then becomes clear that, when it comes to writing, two heads really are better than one.

Take another look at your responses to the top ten lists above. Do you notice any trends that indicate conflict between the voices of the left and right sides of the brain? Is one side more like an adult, the other perhaps more childlike in diction, tone, or syntax? Is one side more logical, the other more emotional? Are there differences in the amount of self-judgment allowed by the two voices? In other words, which side kicks you more while you're already down—or are they both fairly adept at pummeling your self-image as a writer?

Remember, it doesn't matter which side of your brain is the more positive, or outspoken, or childlike. When I say "the right brain," I am speaking of the nondominant side of the brain *for most people*. For example, recent research indicates that functions of the left and right brain may be partially reversed in people who experienced early neglect or chronic trauma. Researchers have also found that people who experience chronic, severe stress during early childhood may have less integration (and therefore less cooperation) between the two sides of the brain. However, regardless of the way our brains developed—whether we were raised by wolves or Mother Teresa—we still have to contend with the two voices in our brains, and get them to agree about our writing.

For most writers, here's how it works: One side of us decides to write, so we actually sit down at the computer, but then some unseen force—aka, anxiety—takes over, and suddenly we're either whirling through cyberspace, glued to HBO with a box of doughnuts, or carving out last week's fossilized spaghetti lodged between the leaves of the dining room table. The write-or-flight challenge has begun—and guess which option we've chosen?

But wait—I'm getting ahead of the game here. What I've just said pertains to the fact that you have already tried to start writing. What if you can't even bring yourself to sit down and face the blank page or the blinking cursor? What if both feel more like intimidation than invitations?

This brings me to another top ten list. Since we can honestly rename the previous list "Top Ten Reasons to Avoid *Publishing*," this next one explores how the two sides of the brain react to the actual *process of writing.* Again, respond instinctively without pausing, first with your dominant hand, then with your other hand.

Dominant Hand
Top Ten Reasons to Avoid the Process of Writing

__10. I never get time alone to write.
__ 9. I hate being alone.
__ 8. I squander my time alone on meaningless activity.
__ 7. I feel like I have nothing to say.
__ 6. I have so much to say, but I don't know how to say it.
__ 5. I don't know where to start.
__ 4. I don't know where the novel/chapter/story/essay/ poem goes next.
__ 3. I shouldn't have to revise.
__ 2. I hate the process of revising.
__ 1. I don't know when to stop revising.

Nondominant Hand
Top Ten Reasons to Avoid the Process of Writing

__10. I never get time alone to write.
__ 9. I hate being alone.
__ 8. I squander my time alone on meaningless activity.
__ 7. I feel like I have nothing to say.
__ 6. I have so much to say, but I don't know how to say it.
__ 5. I don't know where to start.
__ 4. I don't know where the novel/chapter/story/essay/ poem goes next.

___ 3. I shouldn't have to revise.

___ 2. I hate the process of revising.

___ 1. I don't know when to stop revising.

When I peruse my responses to this exercise, I recognize my inner conflict. My dominant hand checked off number 8 (I squander my time on meaningless activity), number 6 (I have so much to say, but I don't know how to say it), and number 5 (I don't know where to start).

In contrast, my nondominant hand checked off number 10 (I never get time alone to write) and number 7 (I feel like I have nothing to say). Interestingly, my nondominant hand also checked off number 5 (I don't know where to start).

I suppose I should be happy that both sides of my brain agree that "I don't know where to start," but that isn't much consolation when I'm chasing my tail instead of writing a novel. However, through the bi-vocal approach, I have learned to write in spite of this cacophony of thoughts from the two sides of my brain.

The Right to Write

Right about now, you're probably wondering how these two sides of your brain can come up with such intense, or intensely different, responses. Where do these voices come from? For most of us, these voices are an amalgamation of every voice we've ever heard. They are the internalized voices of our caretakers, parents, grandparents, siblings, teachers, coaches, neighbors, clergy, spouse—anyone who's had an impact on us. If we haven't yet shaken them off, now is the time to ditch them.

No matter what anyone else says, you do have the right to write.

It's like breathing, Denise Levertov had said. And she was right. If you are a writer at heart, you need to express yourself to feel fully alive. If you don't write, then something might go unsaid—and you'll remain hidden. Hiding provides safety, of course, but it also keeps you from knowing yourself—which may be the point. We all have parts of our past, or present, that we'd rather not own. When I think about how many years I had writer's block—how many years I avoided knowing myself—I am reminded of Ray Bradbury's wise words from *Zen in the Art of Writing*: "I finally figured out that if you are going to step on a live mine, make it your own. Be blown up, as it were, by your *own* delights and despairs."

If you can accept yourself, with all of your quirks and awful experiences, at least then you have a buffer zone between you and the critics, whether they sit onboard the *New York Times Book Review* or at the helm of your very own Family-of-Origin's Sinking Ship of Dysfunction. Either one is enough to drown the most talented writer. That is why it is crucial that you jettison their voices, and listen to yours—both of them. By listening to both sides of your brain, you can begin to accept yourself, as a person and as a writer.

As you complete the following exercise, notice what happens when you switch hands. Try to listen to what each of your voices has to say.

Parallel Monologue

> Dominant Hand
> When I think about being a writer, I feel:_____

> Nondominant Hand
> When I think about being a writer, I feel:_____

Today, I had divergent responses to this parallel monologue: "good" (dominant hand) and "nervous" (nondominant hand)—but I'm still writing!

If either of your responses reveal conflict or anxiety, relax—it's normal. By definition, anxiety is a signal from the brain that we are under threat. Think about it: If a rabid tiger is poised to pounce on you, your right brain will activate a fire hose of adrenaline to propel you as far away as possible. Similarly, if there is a threat to our self-esteem—the red pen of an editor, the critical eye of our readers—then our right brain will release stress hormones to remind us that we can always rely on our fight-or-flight reaction for survival.

As writers, we are exhorted to stay and fight the fight: *Write no matter how lousy you feel about it.* On the other hand, if we take flight from the writing process, we can do just about anything else on the planet: watch inane television, check e-mail, eat junk food, smoke cigarettes, inhale coffee, balance the checkbook, clean the kitchen—you name it, but none of it will produce the Great American Novel. The obvious choice is to write in spite of our internal jitters. So why don't more of us choose this option?

The answer to this question may be explained by the results of recent brain research, which has revealed a third option that precedes the fight-or-flight response: the *freeze* response. In other words, before the sympathetic nervous system (which is ruled by the right side of the brain) triggers the fight-or-flight response, there can be a period of time when we feel immobilized. Reptiles, for example, will freeze by playing dead to avoid predators. Now, this may work for Rosie the Rattlesnake, but it won't work for Walter the Writer. This is exactly what classic writer's block feels like: At the very moment when you want to write, you just can't. The blank page or the blinking cursor might as well be a predator.

The way out of this freezing process is through the right side of the brain. The right brain controls the biochemistry of emotions—that includes our all-time favorite, anxiety—and it also controls the way we react to our own biochemistry. However, by accessing the right side of the brain, we can actually choose our moods. So the next time you say, "I have to be in the mood to write," Chapter 5 of this book can show you how to attain that mood—what researcher Dr. Robert Thayer calls a state of "calm-energy," the ideal state for motivation and concentration.

Of course, as if we aren't stymied enough, the right brain also controls our "all-or-nothing" thinking patterns. That's the side of the brain moaning, *"I need a big block of time to write, and since I don't have it, why bother?"* The right brain is also the one lamenting, *"I get completely overwhelmed thinking about writing an entire book, so I don't even try!"* This type of thinking can freeze our creativity instantly. The right brain is also the searching side of the brain—it seeks to satisfy cravings, to find gratification in what we do, and instantly heads for pleasure and away from pain (read: anxiety). For all these reasons and many more, we need to listen to the right side of the brain.

In the following chapters, you can discover what the right brain has to say—and how to write in spite of the fight. If you're frozen and not yet ready to write, then you might as well find out why, and what to do about it. By reading this book, you are implicitly giving yourself permission to write.

Part I of this book utilizes the bi-vocal approach to help you create the essential components of "the writer's life." Part II applies the bi-vocal approach to the steps of the writing process. Part III offers you a ten-day plan to absorb the bi-vocal approach into your lifestyle. And because I know you're not going to tape this book to your forehead, you'll find the main charts for the bi-vocal approach in the appendix as a "to-go" order of motivation—so you can write whenever, and wherever, you feel like it.

Because if you don't, something might go unsaid.

CHAPTER 2

the all-or-nothing writer:

how to stop feeling overwhelmed

Every writer I know has trouble writing.

—Joseph Heller

I love being a writer.
What I can't stand is the paperwork.

—Peter De Vries

Supply and Demand

Like barnacles on a sinking ship, we cling to the myth that we can complete an entire writing project in one sitting—and that includes novels. If we can't do it all at once, then why bother?

On the other hand, most of us still need that day job. We have trouble scrounging half an hour for lunch, let alone gleaning an hour for writing. Immersed in lives of quiet desperation, we crave a total escape in order to write—as if writing cannot possibly be a part of our everyday lives. We yearn for that week in the mountains, that month in a cabin—even a seedy hotel room across town would do, as long as we didn't have to attend to duties like paying bills, laundry, phone calls, and relationships. When it comes to our writing (and most everything else), it's all or nothing at all.

This chapter demystifies the writing process by showing us that writing can indeed be a part of our everyday lives. We'll discover how and why this all-or-nothing pattern develops in the right side of the brain—and, by using the bi-vocal approach, how to convince the right brain to change this pattern.

The right brain craves instant gratification: *Writing tasks should be completed Perfectly, Instantly, and Effortlessly* (dare I say, easy as *PIE*?). The right brain views any given task as a whole, and has difficulty understanding that tasks can be divided into more manageable subtasks. In this chapter, we'll learn how to challenge these unrealistic expectations by working with—not against—the mysterious right side of the brain.

When it comes to the demanding right side of the brain, here's the key: *Don't deny it, supply it.*

All or Nothing at All

So, now that you've balanced your checkbook, made seven phone calls, checked your e-mail, dashed out for a double espresso latte, and turned on your computer, the only thing you feel like doing is running away. Maybe you do just that. Or, perhaps because you know this is your only writing time this week, you stay there, but no writing occurs. You may sit at your desk, biting your nails, smoking cigarettes, and/or cruising through cyberspace.

Either way, when it comes to writing, you're immobilized. This would be the "nothing" part of the all-or-nothing syndrome.

As mentioned in Chapter 1, the right side of the brain is the command center for the so-called sympathetic nervous system (which doesn't seem at all sympathetic when we're paralyzed by writer's block). When we feel stress or anxiety about the writing process, the sympathetic nervous system triggers the fight-or-flight response—which, for the purposes of this book, I have dubbed the "write-or-flight response."

But remember the freeze response, which may precede the write-or-flight response? Perhaps it's no coincidence that many writers will say that being blocked makes them feel like their creativity is frozen. All we have to do is determine what's threatening us, and we'll stop being frozen. The problem is that *we* are what's threatening us, as the right side of the brain will be glad to inform us, if only we would ask.

This, of course, comprises the "all" part of the all-or-nothing syndrome. Listen closely: Here's what the right side of the brain will tell you.

"I need a big block of time to write."

"I'm totally overwhelmed even thinking about this writing project."

"I need instant gratification—I want this all written *now*."

"I'm hungry/thirsty/tired, and I don't feel like sitting here all day."

In other words, the more primal right side of the brain wants to write instantly, totally, perfectly—without having to revise—and it wants to be satisfied with whatever you might be craving at any given moment. Accordingly, the right brain is responsible for that well-worn path to the refrigerator, and it will veer toward anything that will alleviate our anxiety about writing (e.g., junk food, cigarettes, computer solitaire, you name it).

Batteries Not Included

When I sit down to write, sometimes my brain feels like a dead battery, even though I know I'm creative, I know that I'm a published author, and I know that I have something to say.

On the other hand, given what I now know about myself—and the writing process—I am keenly aware that, when it comes to motivation, nobody told us about the fine print: *Batteries not included.*

What You See Is What You Get

In an ideal world, batteries would be included. Recent brain research explored by Dr. Allan Schore shows that our motivational templates are formed during the first few years of life, and that our "batteries" are fueled by unconditional love.

In an ideal world, according to experts such as Colin Murray Parkes, we all would have had perfect parents and childhood caretakers, who gave us unconditional love from the moment we hit the planet.

They would not have been stressed-out, sleep-deprived neophyte parents still reeling from the flaws in their own caretakers' misguided behaviors.

Our caretakers would have consistently mirrored love in their eyes to ensure we felt loved. None of them would have had postpartum depression, or unhappy marriages, or dead-end jobs, or health problems, or two other small children—anything that could have taken away their ability to attend to us in a consistent, reliable, and loving manner.

And what does all this *Touched by an Angel* parenting have to do with writer's block? Let's take an example of someone who did not get this type of early childhood caretaking and find out why she never seemed to have the right kind of "batteries" to create the life she needed as a writer.

Nora, an office manager who wanted to be a writer, presented with the classic symptoms of procrastination and writer's block. Her house was cluttered, her dietary habits were erratic, she was always running late, she rarely relaxed, and, of course, she never had time to write. Whenever she would try to organize her life so that she could make time to write, she would find herself either paralyzed or frantic—and sometimes both.

What Nora couldn't possibly understand was the fact that, like so many of us, the right side of her brain had been programmed for this state of imbalance during her first few years of life. And when I say "programmed," I mean biochemically.

According to Dr. Allan Schore, our templates for motivation are formed within the first few years of life—a time when the right side of the brain is dominant for everyone. (It's the nonverbal side of the brain, so before full use of language kicks in, the right brain rules.) The delicate balance in the biochemistry of an infant's brain is stimulated by input from caregivers. Every time the child sees love in the caretaker's eyes, that child's right brain will release mood-enhancing neurotransmitters, such as endorphins, serotonin, and dopamine—precisely what is needed in later life for focus and accomplishment.

Ideally, the caregivers will provide the child with appropriate love, emotional stimulation, and consistent, reliable guidance and reassurance, and the child's neural network will develop normally. For example, the neural pathways for dopamine—a brain chemical essential for concentration and motivation—are established by age two. However, many things can go wrong, and the child's brain chemistry can go awry.

Here's how it works: The right side of the brain, which is dominant for controlling the biochemistry of emotion, is also dominant for interpreting visual stimulation. If the caretaker's face reflects strong positive emotions such as love, joy, or excitement, this will stimulate the infant's right brain to release CRF (corticotrophin-releasing factor), which in turn stimulates the infant's sympathetic nervous system.

During infancy, the sympathetic nervous system is supposed to be dominant. This "fight-or-flight" division of the autonomic nervous system activates our heart rate and other vital signs to prepare for responding to an intense stimulus.

Well, we don't call them *new*borns for nothing. When you've just hit the planet, everything is new and intense and interesting, so just about anything can evoke excitement in a baby. The aptly named "sympathetic" nervous system knows that babies are supposed to be excited about having a life!

Healthy caregivers would respond to the child by mirroring the baby's joy and excitement. Alternatively, they would also notice if the child appeared agitated from overstimulation and would provide soothing reassurance, rather than more excitement.

But this phase of eternal excitement can't go on forever. A toddler who is excited about everything is a child in danger. As the child becomes more mobile, he or she begins to explore the environment. When the child tries to explore items like Drano, or reaches for a light socket, the ideal caregiver will respond with a warning, then reassurance. The child's excitement is dimmed as the parasympathetic nervous system takes over. Like a "paramedic" in an emergency, the parasympathetic nervous system tells the child to slow down and calm down.

To ensure the child's survival, the parasympathetic nervous system gradually becomes dominant sometime between the ages of ten and eighteen months. For example, one study by S. R. Tulkin and J. Kagan monitored maternal behaviors toward toddlers between the ages of ten and twelve months. The mothers' behaviors involved some form of affection, playing, or caregiving 90 percent of the time. Only 5 percent of the mothers' behaviors involved prohibiting something the toddler was trying to do.

However, in a study by T. G. Power and M. L. Chapieski, mothers of toddlers ages eleven to seventeen months expressed prohibitions about the child's behavior an average of once every nine minutes! So much for the bliss of parenthood.

At this age, the child is struggling with society's demands for impulse control and delayed gratification. The caregiver must switch from simply being a caretaker to a socialization agent as well. A certain amount of "socialization shame" is generated by the caregiver's admonitions (for example, "Don't hit your brother"), and the child learns to behave appropriately with others.

However, if this occurs more often than not, there may be trouble in toddler paradise. When the child rarely sees joy in the caretaker's face, but instead sees constant disapproval, the child feels an overload of unhealthy shame. Researchers such as U. Lundberg and M. Frankenhauser have shown that shame stimulates the parasympathetic nervous system. Like an actor in a bad episode of *Cops,* when a child feels shame, the body yells "Stop!"

However, once the child is out of danger, the healthy caregiver will then return to a loving attitude while reassuring the toddler that all is well. The positive caretaker, who knows that crying over spilled milk only makes it go sour, does not remain angry but instead conducts "interactive repair" by reassuring the child. The child's shame, which had stimulated the parasympathetic nervous system, has now been "metabolized," and the toddler goes back, eventually, to the excitement generated by the sympathetic nervous system when another joyful experience occurs.

In this ideal scenario, the child develops a healthy balance between the sympathetic and parasympathetic nervous systems. Eventually, the child learns to self-regulate, and, as a result, the child develops a healthy balance among the brain chemicals needed in later life for motivation and concentration (particularly dopamine, serotonin, and endorphins).

But that doesn't mean the child's caretakers were so balanced and excited about life. For example, many new mothers have postpartum depression, and they may suffer for up to a year or longer. Unless these mothers get treatment, the mirroring they offer to their infants isn't exactly going to jump-start those babies—or their sympathetic nervous systems—for life. According to research discussed by Dr. Allan Schore, if the mother is emotionally or physically unavailable, the infant's parasympathetic nervous system will be prematurely activated by a sense of shame at having been "abandoned." Research by experts such as P. V. Trad and K. Tennes shows that this and other forms of attachment bond interruptions create "shame distress" and separation stress, which increases the infants' stress hormones such as cortisol, which in turn may decrease levels of dopamine.

Think about your parents' ability to mirror healthy emotions when you were an infant. What was going on in their worlds that may have caused them to offer you that mirror used by Cinderella's stepmother instead of the one cherished, albeit underwater, by the Little Mermaid? What could have made them ignore you, or habitually exhibit facial expressions of anxiety, anger, grief, or contempt? (Hint: conditions like undiagnosed depression,

AD/HD, anxiety, divorce, financial stress, chronic illness, World War II, Vietnam—you name it.)

Most parents would not have known that an infant would absorb these emotions like a tiny sponge. Any number of problems—including caring for their other children—could have prevented parents from responding appropriately in terms of mirroring a baby's excitement and joy. And if the baby was clearly agitated or crying incessantly, could these same stressors have kept them from soothing that baby?

Even if our childhood caretakers asked the question, "*What does the baby need?*" how often did they answer it *correctly*, let alone do something about it? They were probably busy obeying the Unofficial Parenting Rules of their time—which until recently entailed erroneous statements like, "As long as he's not crying, it's okay to just leave him alone" or, "Let the baby cry; it's good for her lungs." As long as the baby had been fed and diapered, our parents probably figured they'd done their job and could put up their feet and watch *Jeopardy*.

In other words, they were having a life that was typical of the times. With the human condition limiting our caretakers' lives, most of us didn't get the ideal balance of stimulation and consistent reassurance that we needed as infants. As a result, most of us didn't get the ideal balance between our sympathetic and parasympathetic nervous systems.

And we still don't have it.

What You Feel Is What You Get

Let's go back to Nora. She had been raised by a self-absorbed mother, an absentee father (a workaholic surgeon), and an easily agitated nanny who used harsh physical discipline, and Nora soon began to realize that she couldn't focus on her writing because both her sympathetic and parasympathetic nervous systems had been overly activated. Like any other child, Nora craved her parents' affection and protection, and when she didn't get it, she would have felt anxious—her sympathetic fight-or-flight system would have been activated. However, her shame from being ignored by them simultaneously would have activated her parasympathetic nervous system's shutdown mode. While her heart was racing— even infants can sense whether a caretaker is reliable and will ensure the child's survival—she would also be immobilized by shame.

A child who is "scared stiff" with a racing heart is in an unhealthy state of imbalance between the two parts of the autonomic nervous system. Like so many people, Nora had developed an insecure attachment style with her caregivers. According to Dr. Allan Schore, insecure attachment is associated with (1) extremely high or extremely low levels of arousal in the sympathetic and parasympathetic nervous systems, (2) negative emotions, and (3) distracted attention.

On the other hand, a secure attachment style is associated with (1) moderate, balanced levels of arousal in the sympathetic and parasympathetic nervous systems, (2) positive emotions, and (3) focused attention.

When I explained all this, Nora could see why, when it came to her writing, she would freeze, even though she experienced intense internal anxiety. At twenty-seven, she still had an imbalance in her biochemistry. She would do nothing, and feel miserable. Or she would fritter away the weekend on menial tasks or meaningless activity, thereby dissipating her anxiety about not writing. Sound familiar?

Then, sometimes, she would swing into overdrive and stay up late to finish a task—usually unrelated to her writing. Although she was exhausted and ashamed from living in this all-or-nothing mode, Nora didn't want to give it up. The thought of accomplishing tasks in small steps was irritating. She couldn't imagine how so many small steps could actually add up to something big—like the novel she'd been thinking about for years.

Splitting into Infinity

I explained to Nora that this all-or-nothing nemesis was not only biochemical—swinging in and out of the sympathetic and parasympathetic nervous systems without any sense of balance— but it was also psychological.

When children are faced with an intolerable set of emotions, they will engage in a defense mechanism called "splitting," which, according to psychologists such as Dr. Stephen Johnson, may be the precursor to an all-or-nothing dichotomous thinking style. Essentially, toddlers are not able yet to reconcile anxiety-producing behaviors in their caretakers. The children's immature and highly emotional right brain cannot understand that their caretakers may just be good people going through bad times. To rectify this confusion, the child will split the caretaker into two separate selves, so the "bad" side of the caretaker can be ignored. The "all-good Mommy/Daddy" (the one who gives positive attention) is cherished, while the "all-bad Mommy/Daddy" (the one who gives very little or very negative attention) can be discarded.

If nobody taps us on the shoulder to explain why our caretakers were so flawed, in later life this splitting pattern can translate into all-or-nothing thinking. In other words, I am "all-good" if I complete the task totally, instantly, and perfectly—and I am "all-bad" if I don't. Since it's impossible to reach any goals this way, what do we do?

Nothing.

Nada.

Zippo.

This means we are not "all-good," so we end up feeling "all-bad" most of the time, which means we feel shame, which means we are activating our parasympathetic nervous system so it can shout *"Stop!"* every time we try to accomplish anything. We then feel the distress caused by shame, get a rush of cortisol, which aggravates the "write-or-flight" response, and end up feeling too anxious to write. Or, alternatively—like the reptile who freezes and "plays dead" to avoid a threat—we may also feel too paralyzed to write as we face the threat to our self-esteem inherent in that "all-bad" feeling that wells up when we can't "do it all" in one sitting.

So much for self-motivation.

Living Half a Life: The Biochemistry of Writer's Block

In spite of all this biochemical chaos, we can exert control over our brains—and our ability to focus in order to write. Although we'll explore this more in Chapter 5, let's just say for right now that it's important to be aware of how "activated" we are when we try to write.

One easy way to grasp your current level of activation would be to choose among the four mood states that Dr. Robert Thayer presents in *The Origin of Everyday Moods*. After extensive research, Thayer explores what he calls "calm-energy" as the ideal motivational state. However, he points out that most of us alternate between bouts of "tense-tired" and "tense-energy" moods—and we rarely allow ourselves the luxury of genuine relaxation when we are in the "calm-tired" mood.

We need moderate arousal of the sympathetic nervous system to feel energy, and moderate arousal of the parasympathetic nervous system to feel calm. But since our systems are out of balance, we have difficulty attaining the calm-energy mood.

What this translates into is a frenetic, disorganized approach to living half a life. As you can see from the following table I've constructed, this pattern is biochemical, cognitive, and behavioral—and if we add in Dr. Robert Thayer's research—mood-related.

The Biochemistry of Motivation: Don't Just Do Something, Stand There!

Activation in Central Nervous System	Cognitive	Behavioral	Thayer's Moods
High parasympathetic arousal	Freeze! Do *nothing*	Immobilized	Tense-tired
High sympathetic arousal	Gotta do it *all* now	Frantic activity for deadline	Tense-energy
High sympathetic + High parasympathetic arousal	Gotta do it *all* now, but I can't	Anxiety + do unrelated tasks	Tense-energy
Moderate sympathetic+ Moderate parasympathetic arousal	I can have balance	Do part of task, then relax	Calm-energy, calm-tired

In order to release the shame attached to writer's block, it's helpful to acknowledge the strong possibility that these patterns were set in motion—biochemically—long before we could have ever controlled them. If we developed less than optimal arousal levels in our sympathetic/parasympathetic nervous systems due to insecure attachment styles with our parents, it's likely that they did with their parents, too. According to Mary Ainsworth, some researchers have found that 75 percent of women and 69 percent of men will re-create the same attachment patterns that they had with their parents when it comes to interacting with their own children.

So, human nature being what it is, we could probably trace these patterns back through the generations, all the way back to the amoebas, and perhaps that might help some of us let go of our shame about writer's block triggered by a central nervous system gone awry. As a matter of fact, researchers such as Mary Main have found that when we can accept the fact that these feelings of shame may be a result of the way we were treated by our parents rather than an inherent part of our character, we are much less likely to repeat the same patterns with our own children, and we can move on. By doing this, we can release the shame attached to our lack of motivation. Remember: Shame activates the parasympathetic nervous system, which means: *Stop—slow down, do nothing until the situation is stable.*

Now that we know why we might get anxious or freeze up at the sight of a blinking cursor, let's explore some techniques for releasing our creative energies into a state of flow.

Easy as Pie

Okay, so the right brain wants everything done perfectly, instantly, effortlessly. And that is exactly how we're going to change our writing process.

By definition, writing shall become a chunk of time, not a chunk of written output. Your right brain will be happy that your writing will now be done:

> **Perfectly**—all you have to do is put in the time.
>
> **Instantly**—all you have to do is spend five minutes with your Muse.
>
> **Effortlessly**—all you have to do is eek out an SFD.

What's an SFD? That's my abbreviation for a marvelous phrase presented by Anne Lamott in *Bird by Bird*. As a child, when her brother had to write a book report about birds, he was overwhelmed. He'd asked his father just how this could be done, and the father had replied, "Bird by bird." In exploring this and other notions about writing, Lamott tells us that there is no such thing as a *first draft*. Instead, she says, there are only "shitty first drafts." By definition, a first draft is supposed to be, shall we say, lousy.

That's where the "effortless" part comes in. If all you have to do is slap an SFD on the page, which can be effortless: Mistakes are welcome. Here's a page from one of my many SFDs:

for ch. 10 — WB

→ Right about now, you're prob. thinking, [ital →] Why bother — I'm not going to finish a ~~novel~~ in 10 days?
(diss report)

And you're right — but you might start [ital] a novel / diss / report in 10 days.

And in 10 more days, you could be even further along in the process of complet'g your wr. project.

~~Think back to something you've~~

But right now you ~~prob.~~ feel frustrated because, like the rest of us, you want it all done now, perfectly, of course — even tho' you know it's one step at a time.

So let's do a flash forward.
~~Think back to something you've~~

On the other hand, how many babies do you know who've taken their first step, + then sat down and moped for the rest of his/her life because

Much Ado about Something

Before you begin to change your writing process, let me remind you to go easy on yourself. Keep in mind that the more challenging and uncomfortable your childhood years were, the more likely it is that you may struggle with the write-or-flight response. Researchers such as Martin Teicher have found that many people who were exposed to chronic or extreme stress during early childhood (a mother with postpartum depression; a father with AD/HD resulting in poor impulse control and rage reactions; child abuse/neglect) have less integration between the right and left hemispheres of the brain. Additionally, other researchers such as Douglas Bremner and Gerardo Villarreal have found that some people who were abused as children have shrinkage in the hippocampus, which means less control over the fight-or-flight response. In other words, since chronic stress during the first three years of life affects brain development, those of us who weren't brought up on the set of *The Brady Bunch* may have more difficulty managing the classic fight-or-flight response—which unfortunately means we are more likely to take flight, rather than write.

However, there are ways to help us write while at the same time addressing our needs for instant gratification, perfectionism, and a sense of control. Here's what we'll use in this chapter to jump-start our writing process:

> The To-Do (or Not-To-Do) List—a list of choices
> Task-shaping—a way to manage writing subtasks
> Task-sprinting—a way to accomplish writing subtasks
> Reward-shaping—a way to reinforce our writing process.

As we explore these techniques, keep in mind that not only does the right side of the brain control the fight-or-flight response, but it is also the reward center of the brain. Constantly on the prowl for that next blast of mood-enhancing dopamine—our so-called reward neurotransmitter—the right brain has difficulty engaging in hard work without immediate gratification. The right brain can't sit for hours, typing away, only to find at the end of the day that the entire writing project is not finished!

In this section, we will discover how to cajole the right brain into following the left brain's logical lead by learning the fine art of "task-sprinting": dividing writing tasks into manageable parts (spend twenty minutes on an essay's rough outline on Tuesday, five minutes of writing part one of the outline on Wednesday, etc.), and immediately giving the right brain the reward it craves (reading the magazines on your own coffee table, checking e-mail, racking up twenty-minute blocks of time toward seeing a movie).

Although we may balk at the notion of providing external rewards for the intrinsically rewarding act of writing, we'll soon see that these external rewards are precisely what the right brain indulges in anyway once it yanks us away from writing, so we might as well short-circuit such self-sabotage and get what we want *as part of the writing process*—guilt-free. (More about this later—I know that, as a writer, you are not going to stop right now and brainstorm a list of rewards.)

By definition, writing now becomes a process, *not a product*. Just the mere fact that you put in twenty minutes of writing time means that you have achieved success, regardless of the quality (or length) of your "SFD."

The To-Do (or Not-To-Do) List

Most people either don't bother with to-do lists, or they make lists and then ignore them—or lose them. Now, pardon me for sounding like a shrink here, but do you suppose the right brain has anything to do with this? Maybe, just maybe, disregarding or losing to-do lists is the right brain's way of saying to the left brain: "I don't want to do this."

Well, if that's the case, let's go ahead and acknowledge that both sides of the brain have the right to vote on this. We're going to use the To-Do (or Not-To-Do) List, because it's important to acknowledge that it's just as much of a choice *not to do* a writing task as it is to do it.

In other words, the "to-do" option means we'll choose to write, while the "not-to-do" option means we'll career off to the nearest Starbucks for a double mocha java and probably hit Krispy Kreme on the way back. On the other hand, while your right brain got to choose the "not-to-do" option, you just may choose the "to-do" option once you're magnetized back to your computer again.

The following list includes the time you estimate for the task, as well as the actual time spent on the task. Reward time should be equal to the actual time, if possible. Otherwise, go for half the actual time spent on the task—but no less.

And remember: If a task takes longer than you expected, it's still a win-win, because that simply means you get more reward time!

To-Do (or-Not-To-Do) List

Estimated Time	Task	Actual Time	Reward Time
_____	1. _____ _____	____	____
_____	2. _____ _____	____	____
_____	3. _____ _____	____	____
_____	4. _____ _____	____	____
_____	5. _____ _____	____	____

Maybe you listed tasks like these: *create a writing area, buy a new computer, start my novel.* Each one of these tasks can be broken down into subtasks, all of which contribute to shaping your final goal. For example, let's do some "task-shaping" for the goal of *starting your novel.*

Task-Shaping

Estimated Time	Subtask	Actual Time	Reward Time
_____	1. Character sketch of protagonist	____	____
_____	2. Character sketch of antagonist	____	____
_____	3. Decide on 3-act structure	____	____

_____	4. Write opening scene	____	____
_____	5. Write closing scene	____	____
_____	6. Write the epilogue	____	____
_____	7. Write the most angry scene	____	____
_____	8. Write the most happy scene	____	____
_____	9. Write the climactic scene	____	____
_____	10. Write any scene	____	____

Now you're starting to see that you have choices. You can start anywhere, and patch it all together later. When I'm working on a novel, I've often gone off for a cup of tea, between clients at work, and spent twenty minutes writing whatever scene just pops into my head once I sit down. (We'll discuss this "patchwork quilt" method of writing further in Chapter 6.)

Task-Sprinting

Now we're going to try a technique I call "task-sprinting": making a commitment to engage in writing for a short time, based on your mood at the moment. Notice that this next chart offers your right brain the choice to "try" a snippet of writing, and that reward time is included as well. I call this the "PC" approach to engaging the childlike right brain. And I don't mean "politically correct."

Here's how it works. What happens when you ask a child to clean his or her room? The child runs for the hills, of course, because (1) kids don't like being ordered to do something, and (2) cleaning is boring. Like any child, the right brain needs to know that it has a Choice (whether to try the task or not, and for how many minutes), and that a task can be Playful (just clean *half* of the room today, plus you get a "reward"). For simplicity, I've listed Dr. Robert Thayer's four mood states (from his book *The Origin of Everyday Moods*) in the following chart, but we'll expand on this in Chapter 5. Imagine that you have a few minutes right now to write, and see what happens when you fill in the chart.

Task/Activity:_____

Current mood:

___tense-tired   ___tense-energy   ___calm-energy   ___calm-tired

I'll try it for:

___5 minutes   ___10 minutes   ___15 minutes   ___20 minutes

Actual time:

___5 minutes   ___10 minutes   ___15 minutes   ___20 minutes

Reward time:

___5 minutes   ___10 minutes   ___15 minutes   ___20 minutes

You many want to go ahead and try a bit of writing right now. And keep in mind that once you have used this chart, you can sign on for another block of time—but be sure to note your mood first, and be ready to get credit for time served. (Though you may profess your love of writing, it's still hard work.)

Reward: Creative Spirit, Dead or Alive

If you've already brainstormed a list of rewards for your task-sprinting, then you may want to skip this section. However, if your writing task is one that is aversive (oh, let's say an annual report, perhaps a dissertation), then rewards are essential in cajoling the right brain to cooperate.

One of the first questions I ask my clients is "When was the last time you had fun, *guilt-free*?"

Usually, there's a long pause—too long—and then the inevitable response: "Well, I did something fun awhile ago, but I felt guilty about it afterward, and the whole time I was thinking about all the things I should've been doing." Maybe they went to the movies, but the whole time they were gazing at Brad Pitt or Julia Roberts, they were riding waves of guilt and not really enjoying the movie. Even if they did enjoy the movie, as soon as the credits rolled, they were hit with a wave of dread as they remembered how they'd have to pay for taking this time off for not-so-good-behavior.

Having fun is not valued in our society. We deprive ourselves of any enjoyment in life because we haven't finished—or started—any number of tasks. We feel like we have to *earn* the right to have fun. Writers are especially adept at self-deprivation: We have to feel guilty for procrastinating like everybody else, plus we get an extra dose of guilt—daily—for not writing.

Well, for the right side of the brain, this simply will not do. As writers, particularly when we are working on an arduous assignment, we need to learn how to do two things:

1. List all those things we'd like to do but never let ourselves do (or even if we *do* do them, we don't let ourselves truly enjoy them).

2. Do them—guilt-free.

The right brain won't argue. Just think: For every twenty minutes you spend chasing your tail around that impossibly overwhelming novel, you'll get twenty minutes of "reward time" to—imagine this—actually read someone else's novel, just for pleasure.

No matter what you do in terms of your writing, you'll get credit for time served. Each twenty-minute block of "task-sprinting" counts toward something: twenty minutes of a movie, $2 toward a new CD, $10 toward that weekend getaway. And the good news is, if it takes you longer than expected, who cares? You'll just get more reward time or reward money.

We expect ourselves to be calm when we approach our writing, but we're not, or else we would have done it by now. Since we're going to be riddled with anxiety anyway, we might as well get "paid" for it—and make it part of the process of reaching our goals.

When I ask clients to brainstorm a set of rewards, I am always aware that one person's reward may be another person's misery. Some people like to make phone calls as a reward, while others find that the telephone is one of their worst enemies. The key is to jot down, as quickly as possible, all the activities you wish you had time for, but never let yourself do. Just in case you're feeling blocked, following is a list of guilt-free rewards, both short-term and long-term. Glance through the items listed, and then feel free to write in your choices in the blank lists that follow.

Short-Term *Guilt-Free* Rewards

1. Checking e-mail
2. Phone call to friend
3. Lying in a hammock
4. Reading for pleasure
5. Playing with your children
6. Watching a movie
7. Going out to lunch
8. Going for a stroll
9. Going to the beach
10. Reading magazines

Long-Term *Guilt-Free* Rewards

1. Sailing
2. A weekend away
3. Buying a new suit
4. Building something new
5. A two-week trip

Okay, so now it's your turn. Just fill in whatever comes to mind.

Short-Term *Guilt-Free* Rewards

1. _____
2. _____
3. _____
4. _____
5. _____

6. _____
7. _____
8. _____
9. _____
10. _____

Long-Term *Guilt-Free* Rewards

1. _____
2. _____
3. _____
4. _____
5. _____
6. _____
7. _____
8. _____
9. _____
10. _____

Off to See the Muse

As you use these charts, be aware that if you get stuck, it may be because you need to move on to Chapter 3 (when to find time to write during your typical day), Chapter 4 (finding a place to write), and/or Chapter 5 (getting yourself in the mood to write). In Chapters 6 through 9, we'll explore the different stages of writing (starting, continuing, completing, publishing). Finally, in Chapter 10, we'll combine all of these techniques we've explored into one chart—and get you on your Ten-Day Writing Plan at last!

CHAPTER 3

steal this time:

how to live—and write—on
168 hours a week

Writing is a dog's life,

but the only life worth living.

—Gustave Flaubert

I write when I feel like it and wherever I feel like it,

and I feel like it most of the time.

—Jerzy Kosinski

As Time Goes By

This chapter dispels the notion that we can't write until we get that elusive Big Block of Time. For many of us, writing often becomes merely an affair to remember: Like Cary Grant atop the Empire State Building, we'll spend endless hours in our self-imposed rain of reticence just waiting, waiting for the Muse to arrive. Even if we do chance upon some free time, we don't use it for writing. Instead, we make phone calls, check e-mail, balance our checkbooks, scrub hubcaps—any meaningless activity will do—until at last the clock strikes midnight and back down that elevator of despair we go.

In this chapter, we'll learn how to stop dissipating our nervous energy—and squandering precious writing time—on mundane tasks. Instead of trying the usual left-brain time management methods—which most writers resist—we'll explore a more right-brained approach to choosing our writing periods. The right brain bristles at the left brain's logical graph depicting the measly 168 hours we get each week and reacts with disdain—and rebellion— to the left brain's strategy of structuring our time for work, school, meals, household duties, exercise, and, of course, writing.

On the other hand, if we offer the visually dominant right brain first dibs on those 168 hours per week, it is much more likely to cooperate. We'll use colors—rather than words—to engage the nonverbal right brain in the process of choosing the best time of day to write, whether it's once a week or once a day. Remember: It's all about supply and demand. If the right brain—Emperor of Intuition—demands something, and you supply it, then your natural, intuitive writing habits are more likely to surface.

And so will your manuscript.

It's Not about Time, It's about the Time of Day

So what exactly is the best time for your writing? Various theorists and researchers have tried to determine the best time of day for motivation and concentration. For example, Dr. Robert Thayer has conducted research on circadian rhythms—the body's natural daily cycles of energy. He has found that most people get a surge of what he calls "calm-energy"—the ideal motivational state—in the late morning, and sometimes in the early evening. Of course, there are variations to this generic pattern of daily energy rhythms. For example, Dr. Thayer has also found that introverts tend to have more energy earlier in the day, while extroverts tend to have more energy later in the day.

On the other hand, according to endocrinologist and Ayurvedic physician Dr. Deepak Chopra (*Perfect Health*), ancient Hindu texts suggest that we all have three types of energy, with most people being ruled by one or two dominant types: Vata, Pitta, and Kapha, each of which supposedly rules during certain hours of the day. Dr. Chopra suggests using your body type to determine the times of the day for peak energy.

For example, people who are dominantly Vata (prefer spicy foods, tend to be thin, like an ectomorph) may be most energetic from 2 to 6 P.M. and 2 to 6 A.M. People who are ruled more by Pitta (prefer extremely hot or extremely cold foods, tend to be muscular, like the mesomorph) may be most alert from 10 A.M. to 2 P.M. and 10 P.M. to 2 A.M. On the other hand, individuals who are dominantly Kapha (prefer heavier foods, tend to have a solid build, like the endomorph) may be most productive from 6 to 10

A.M. and 6 to 10 P.M. However, we can be out of balance in terms of these three types of "energy"—for example, if a predominantly Pitta person has too much Kapha energy, he or she may feel more sluggish than usual, regardless of the time of day.

Regardless of our beliefs, in terms of body "types" or types of "energy" at various times of the day, we are all unique individuals with widely divergent preferences, life experiences, and responsibilities. How can we each find our individual template for motivation on any given day?

Only the right brain knows for sure. . . .

Why We Detest Time Management

I can hear the gavel pounding as the prison sentence is pronounced: You—Must—Set—Up—a—Schedule. Yes, the right side of the brain would rather run for the hills than face a piece of paper ruled by the worst of all evils: structure.

That's why we shudder at the thought of time management. For many people, setting up a schedule feels like we are somehow being controlled. We look at our lives on paper, segmented into arbitrary blocks of one activity or another, and suddenly life doesn't feel like much fun anymore. Suddenly, we're back in high school, with our days regimented by authority figures who don't care what we feel like doing at any given hour of the day: *Just do it.*

The rebellious right brain responds to this arbitrary structure with not-so-civil disobedience. Instead of writing, the right brain has you whirling through cyberspace, checking your e-mail, dawdling on the phone, dashing out for a coffee, smoking a cigarette, or enduring another round of inane television. In other words, the right side of the brain wants to play. However, the right brain is smart enough to know it isn't going to get away with blatant fun—so it sneaks in *somewhat* enjoyable activities. And by the time the logical left brain kicks in and takes charge again, hours have gone by, with no real work—or genuine fun—to show for it.

The Art of Day-Shaping

Following is a grid depicting the 168 hours we are allotted each week. And, no, we are not going to do time management.

Instead, I'd like you to open a box of crayons, colored markers, or colored pencils—your choice. (If you have none, dash out to buy some—the colors are crucial to this exercise.)

Now, with your nondominant hand, start selecting colors that represent the way you feel at various hours of the day. Don't think about it—just let your nondominant hand drift toward the colors that feel right.

Then, again with your nondominant hand, color in the hours on the following grid.

You may find that you need to blend together several colors for certain hours of the day, but try to get a general feeling for your moods throughout the hours and days of a typical week, and color them in. You may choose to color in just one day, to represent your typical week. Color in as much—or as little—as you please. Remember: This is just for you, and no one else.

Now that you've colored your world, let's take the next step in learning how to shape your day into one that works for you.

Scan the previous chart, and notice any trends. You may intuitively know what each color means to you at different times of the day. (There is no "right" way to interpret the meaning of these colors: Green can be soothing to one person, or it may represent boredom to another person.)

Are there certain times of day—or certain days—when you feel low energy, or especially focused? With your colored time sheet in hand, take a moment to answer the following questions:

Low-Energy Times

Are there certain times of day when you have very little energy or focus?_____

If so, what do you usually do during these times?_____

During these low-energy times, which activities do you try to do, but find that you can't?_____

Are you sabotaging your writing by putting it in a low-energy time slot?_____

Is there a less important activity, or one that requires less focus, that you could do during these low-energy times?_____

High-Energy Times

Are there certain times of day when you're more energized or focused?_____

If so, what do you usually do during these times?_____

Are you giving away your most productive time to someone else?_____

How could you insert your writing into at least part of this time?_____

When people think about what they'd *rather* be doing during their most productive time, they usually get all tangled up in a whirl of shoulds and needs and wants. Let's start with the most important, the ones we most often ignore—what we actually *want*.

List three *wants* (more time for writing, reading, leisure activities, socializing, etc.):

1. _____
2. _____
3. _____

Now, list three *needs* (exercise, grocery shopping, housekeeping, etc.):

Now, list three *necessities* (sleeping, eating, working, etc.):

Let's go back to the first list: wants. Right about now, you're probably thinking, "If I can't get twenty hours a week for writing, why bother?" It's probably true that you may need to work up to the ideal number of hours you can have for your writing, but if you start by stealing back even one hour a week, people who monopolize your other 167 hours a week won't even notice.

So go ahead and list both the ideal *and* minimum number of hours of writing you'd be willing to start with. The idea is to start with any amount of time—even five minutes—but also write down how much you'll eventually get, so the right brain doesn't feel discouraged or deprived. Respond first with your nondominant hand, then switch to your dominant hand and respond again.

Nondominant Hand

My writing time

Ideal amount of time per week   Minimum amount of per week

_____   _____

Dominant Hand

My writing time

Ideal amount of time per week   Minimum amount of per week

_____   _____

Notice that the two sides of your brain probably gave different responses. Mine certainly did. My all-or-nothing right brain (nondominant hand) demanded no less than a full-time job: forty hours per week. If it had to settle for less, the minimum amount of writing time that would be acceptable was twenty hours, your basic half-time job. Nothing less would do.

However, my dominant hand offered different responses. My logical left brain requested twenty-five hours per week for my writing, but it would settle for just one hour for starters.

Therein lies the compromise, so the right and left brain can work as a team. Although my right brain got to pick the colors that helped me determine *which times* each week I'd like to write, my logical left brain is keenly aware of my fluctuating schedule, so the left brain gets to pick *the amount of time* I'll start with in any given week: one hour—and if I get more time for writing, that's gravy.

Notice the trends in your responses to this exercise. Decide which side of the brain offers a more viable minimum/maximum amount of time for writing each week, given your current health, your job, your home life, your schooling, etc.

Now, let's go back to your colored time sheet. If possible, pick the best part of the day for your writing, and fill those in first—even if it's only for the minimum amount of time desired. If your work or home schedule won't yet accommodate this, then pick your second, or even third choice for a time slot—but write in your creativity time first. Be sure to select at least the minimum amount of time you'd like for your writing.

In other words, instead of letting the oh-so-logical left brain write in all those *shoulds* like "work," "sleep," and "chores," let the right brain have first dibs on those 168 hours we get each week, every week. It's the same tactic financial experts recommend for conquering debt: *Pay yourself first.* Once the right brain knows that its writing needs will be met, it will step aside and allow the logical left brain to sort out the rest of the week.

After you've chosen your times for your writing, you can then allow the logical left brain to fill in the hours for everything else. Be careful not to fill up every single hour of the week—the right side of the brain does not like to be hemmed in! Leave space for later decisions that may come up regarding your use of those precious 168 hours each week.

Now that you've colored in your time sheet to reflect the way you feel throughout the day, you may be stunned to see that for years you've probably tried to write at the worst possible time of day, mood-wise, for you. For example, you may or may not know why 3 P.M. is a "brownout" time for you, but you can quickly discern that the sunny yellow of 10 A.M. or the misty blue of 4 P.M. is the best time for you to beckon the Muse.

You have also selected both the *minimum* and the *ideal* amount of writing time each week, so that even if all you get in Week 1 is a mere twenty minutes, the all-or-nothing right brain won't throw a hissy fit once it sees that the ideal amount of writing time will be attained in the near future.

In choosing colors to express the way you feel during different hours of the day, you are asking the highly visual, intuitive, nonverbal right side of the brain which times of the day would be best for your writing. Giving the right brain first dibs on your time is crucial. If you don't, it will just grab the time back anyway: *Hello e-mail, goodbye Great American Novel. . . .*

Remember: When it comes to the right side of the brain, don't defy it—supply it.

Time Management by Intuition

Mon.	Tues.	Wed.	Thurs.	Fri.	Sat.	Sun.
6 A.M.						
7						
8						
9						
10						
11						
12						
1 P.M.						
2						
3						
4						
5						
6						
7						
8						
9						
10						
11						
12						

Wants: _____
Needs: _____

Ideal Time _____

Minimum Time _____

Energy Management by Color

	Mon.	Tues.	Wed.	Thurs.	Fri.	Sat.	Sun.
6 A.M.							
7							
8							
9							
10							
11							
12							
1 P.M.							
2							
3							
4							
5							
6							
7							
8							
9							
10							
11							
12							
1 A.M.							
2							
3							
4							
5							

CHAPTER 4

a clean, well-lighted place to write:

your place or theirs?

All you need is a room without any particular interruptions.

—John Dos Passos

I need noise and interruptions and irritation: irritation and discomfort are a great starter. The loneliness of doing it any other way would kill me.

—Anita Brookner

The actual process of writing . . . demands complete, noiseless privacy, without even music; a baby howling two blocks away will drive me nuts.

—William Styron

The Sounds of Silence

As we all know, writers are not a homogeneous group. Some of us need absolute silence for writing, while others are unnerved by silence and instead crave the sounds of humanity—or even chaos—to achieve creative flow. On the other hand, some of us alternate between craving silence and chaos, depending on our moods or the type of writing task at hand. This explains, at least in part, why we can't seem to find a comfortable place to write. We either choose the wrong setting, or we don't allow ourselves the luxury of having more than one setting, depending on our mood and the type of writing to be done that particular day.

Take the case of Michael, a waiter with a B.A. in English. He worked long hours, and rarely had time to write, but when he did, he seemed to be looking for inspiration in all the wrong places. The library was "too quiet," the local Starbucks was "too sedate," and in his writing studio at home, he felt as if "the walls were closing in" on him. I asked him if he'd ever written successfully, and if so, where. He said the only place where he'd ever been productive was at his sister's kitchen table!

We explored this further, and Michael realized that the raucous comings and goings of his nieces and nephews made him somehow relax. They reminded him of his pleasant childhood memories of growing up in a bustling household with four siblings. It was as if his sensory-dominant right brain needed these familiar sounds to allow the creative process to flow. Michael decided to honor this internal request. He arranged for regular "kitchen table time" at his sister's, and he found two other places to write where he could hear the sounds of children's laughter: the local park, and a seat near the playroom at the local McDonald's.

As this case illustrates, the right side of the brain can be strongly affected by solitude, and for this reason, certain writing projects are better done when we are not alone. Sometimes we may need to write in a café or a bookstore—where we are alone with our work, but can still hear the tinkling of silverware and glasses, the hushed voices of others who may someday pass by with one of *our* books in hand—all in a setting *without* piles of paperwork/Visa bills/chewing gum/tax receipts strewn about layers of legal pads and computer printouts of our latest blasts of dialogue or exposition. This, of course, does not preclude the fact that sometimes we may still crave the familiar clutter of our home-based writing nest.

In other words, sometimes, all the right brain needs to jump-start our writing is a clean, well-lighted place.

And sometimes not.

Clutter, Chaos, and Creativity

Keeping in mind that the right brain is dominant for visual input, in this chapter we'll also explore why setting is just as important during our writing time as it is for that first novel. For example, if your writing area is cluttered—and whose isn't?—then the right brain feels cluttered. Although this ratchets up the level of creativity for a few writers, for most of us, visual clutter creates mental clutter.

As writers, we are curators of the artifacts of our creative outbursts: newspaper clippings riddled with potential characters, plot points jotted on Post-it notes, cocktail napkins sporting our witticisms, dissertation topics scrawled on the back page of a *Time* magazine. As budding—or experienced—writers, we'll etch our ideas onto any surface we can find to preserve those precious blips on the radar screen of our creativity.

This means we end up with a chaotic swirl of papers and found objects littering our desks, dining room tables, pockets, and glove compartments. Additionally, when it comes to organization, most writers are not meticulous about filing. We are "pilers," not filers, because as far as the vision-ruled right brain is concerned, once we file it, it's gone. *If you can't see it, it doesn't exist.* However, when we sit down to write, the highly visual right brain is immediately distracted by all the creative clutter we have accumulated, and our ability to focus on a given writing task literally gets lost in the shuffle. In this chapter, we'll discover how to outsmart—and work with—the right brain's contradictory visual patterns so that our writing time can be used for creating art rather than cursing our self-made Mount Everest of chaos.

Take Five

In considering our different preferences for the setting of our writing arenas, it's important to remember that the right brain is dominant for all sensory input: visual, auditory, tactile, olfactory, and gustatory stimuli. If we pay attention to the five senses, they can serve as allies in creating our ideal place for writing.

Additionally, we need to consider *sensory processing issues.* Our level of adjustment to sensory input will affect our level of comfort with our surroundings. Take, for example, children who are born with "sensory processing disorder" (which, according to experts such as Carol Kranowitz, may be caused by a variety of factors, such as genetics, extreme stress or illness or the ingestion of toxins during pregnancy, birth trauma from an emergency cesarean section, postnatal surgery, or excessive or insufficient sensory stimulation after birth). These children will display an oversensitivity—or an undersensitivity—to bright lights, aversive smells, certain textures of food or clothing, loud noises, or sudden movement. Essentially, they cannot effectively regulate the sensory input going into their brains. However, with professional guidance, these children can often learn how to function more easily in their environments.

Regardless of your level of sensory integration, these same principles apply to the creation of your writing zones—both private and public. You may already know that you need bright light, an uncluttered desk, fresh air, total silence, a good cup of coffee, and a gel ink rollerball pen for that first draft. Or, you may need to write on a laptop computer in a crowded airport—like I used to—full of bustling travelers, loud announcements, stale air, and no-hassle waitresses serving bottomless cups of tea. What you may not know is that you may need different sites for writing on different days, depending on your mood, the type of writing, and whether the left or right side of your brain is calling the shots that day.

Let's do the following parallel monologue to find out what your general preferences are from each side of your brain. We'll start with your preferred level of sensory input, first with the dominant side of your brain, and then with the nondominant side.

Just mark the points on the following continuums that correspond to the intensity of sensory input you need while you are writing. Notice that each of these "Likert scales" offers extremes at both ends of the spectrum, with gradations in between. For example, if you like to write in a subdued café, you might circle the number three in the "auditory stimulation" section.

Dominant Hand

Auditory Stimulation

Quiet   1   2   3   4   5   6   7   8   9   10   Noisy

Visual Stimulation

Spartan area 1   2   3   4   5   6   7   8   9   10 Cluttered area

Plain paper   1   2   3   4   5   6   7   8   9   10 Colored paper
(color:___)

Plain pen/   1   2   3   4   5   6   7   8   9   10 Colored pen/
pencil   pencil(color:___)

Tactile Stimulation

Paper & pen/ 1   2   3   4   5   6   7   8   9   10 Computer
pencil

Olfactory Stimulation

Odorless   1   2   3   4   5   6   7   8   9   10 Strong Smell
(specify:___)

Gustatory Stimulation

Cold liquids   1   2   3   4   5   6   7   8   9   10 Hot liquids
(specify:___)

No food   1   2   3   4   5   6   7   8   9   10 Abundant food
(specify:___)

Now, let's switch hands, and see if the right hand knows what the left hand is *really* doing.

<u>Nondominant Hand</u>

Auditory Stimulation

Quiet   1   2   3   4   5   6   7   8   9   10   Noisy

Visual Stimulation

Spartan area 1   2   3   4   5   6   7   8   9   10 Cluttered area

Plain paper   1   2   3   4   5   6   7   8   9   10 Colored paper
(color:___)

Plain pen/   1   2   3   4   5   6   7   8   9   10 Colored pen/
pencil   pencil(color:___)

Tactile Stimulation

Paper & pen/ 1   2   3   4   5   6   7   8   9   10 Computer
pencil

Olfactory Stimulation

Odorless   1   2   3   4   5   6   7   8   9   10 Strong Smell
(specify:___)

Gustatory Stimulation

Cold liquids 1   2   3   4   5   6   7   8   9   10 Hot liquids
(specify:___)

No food   1   2   3   4   5   6   7   8   9   10 Abundant food
(specify:___)

As you peruse your responses to this exercise, notice any discrepancies between the responses given by the right and left sides of the brain. Perhaps you can see why you may have felt conflicted about what type of writing environment—and props—you need to generate that elusive creative flow.

For example, here are my responses, today, to this exercise. My nondominant hand needed between a 7 and 8 for auditory stimulation, while my dominant hand only checked a 2. This corresponds to my penchant in the past (when I was ruled by my right brain) for writing in noisy cafés and airports, as well as my current preference for quiet cafés and the privacy of my writing studio.

For visual stimulation, my right brain requested an 8 for clutter and a 10 for both colored paper (purple) and colored pens (purple, pink, or blue). In contrast, my left brain requested a 2 for a more spartan environment, a 2 for more plain paper (pastel if colored at all), and an 8 for colored pens (any color). These contrasting responses reflect my need in the past to have *just the right colors* of pen and paper while I wrote in a cyclone of chaos, as opposed to my current preference for a lightly decorated writing studio and more flexible options regarding paper and pens.

In terms of tactile stimulation, my right brain marked a 2 to indicate a strong preference for paper and pen, while my left brain marked between 5 and 6 to reflect my current use of both handwritten and typed manuscripts. In the distant past, when I was convinced that computers would eat my words, I would only use computers as a last resort for the final draft. Now, I usually write manuscripts in longhand first, then type them in as I revise them. However, sometimes I do compose right at the computer, as I'm doing right now.

My responses regarding olfactory stimulation were highly divergent. With my nondominant hand, I checked a 1 for odorless, but with my dominant hand, I checked a 10 for a strong smell of "fresh air." I can see why my right brain would go for "odorless," to ensure that nothing aversive might distract me. On the other hand, my left brain knows that, given the choice, I usually choose to write outdoors rather than indoors.

Finally, in terms of gustatory stimulation, it's clear that the two sides of my brain have their differences. My right brain checked a 1 for cold liquids and 9 for an abundance of food. However, my left brain checked between 3 and 4 for cold liquids, and between 4 and 5 for amount of food. Again, these responses reflect my past and present habits. In the past, I'd absolutely have to have an ice-cold Diet Coke and various snack foods available in order to start writing. Now, I can live with it if my iced green tea drifts to room temperature, and I try to focus on "brain foods" (protein especially) when I need some energy while writing (more about this in Chapter 5).

Since I am keenly aware that the right side of the brain is the repository not only for creativity, but also for sensory input, emotion, negative childhood experiences, and all-or-nothing thinking patterns, I'm not surprised by my responses to this exercise. All I have to do is go traipsing around in that right side of my brain, looking for the door to my creativity, and part of me knows that it may not be the Muse who answers. However, in practicing the techniques in this book, I have learned to brave my own minefields, as Ray Bradbury suggests in *Zen in the Art of Writing*. The discrepancies between the two sides of my brain clearly indicate that my right brain still tends toward extremes, while my left brain is more moderate—and realistic—in setting the standards for my writing environment and all of its props.

As you glance through your responses to this exercise, it may become apparent which side of the brain you need to honor in terms of your sensory preferences while you're writing. For example, you may want to use stepwise vertical files to replace your piles and reduce clutter. These are great for the right side of the brain: As each file is placed in the gradually ascending hierarchy of wire slots, you can still see what you've placed there, even though it has technically been "filed."

These stepwise vertical files are great for larger projects. For example, I have two on my desk right now, one holding files containing Chapters 1 through 5, and the other holding Chapters 6 through 10 of this book. Even though I have technically "filed" all ten chapters, my right brain can still see them all at a glance. It's the beauty of having piles instead of files: They're just vertical piles, instead of horizontal piles. The payoff is that my right brain isn't diverted by the visual chaos of papers askew all over my desk.

However, it's important to remember to be flexible, to allow either side of the brain to rule on any given writing day during any given writing task. For example, yesterday, while I was working on this chapter, I was at home writing on my computer for two hours, and then I started feeling edgy, so I went out to a local diner and continued outlining and writing—by hand—for two hours there.

The trick is to make a decision on what you need for that particular day, and then go for it, rather than sitting immobilized while the right and left brain duke it out. Remember: You need *both* sides of the brain to fight—and conquer—writer's block.

Mirror, Mirror on the Screen: The Problem with Solitude

As writers, we often need solitude in order to concentrate. One day, while writing, I came across a striking symbol of my need to avoid solitude. It was right after I started using my new laptop computer when I first noticed that moving paper clip on the right side of the computer screen. Every now and then—like just now—it moves around a bit, lifts its eyebrows, glances around, but mostly gazes at me while I write.

Somebody at Microsoft is more than a genius. This thing is actually mirroring approval to me. It's giving me what D. W. Winnicott would have called the ability "to be alone in the presence of mother," which is the cornerstone to a sense of security, which in turn engenders the ability to tolerate solitude. This is what we were all *supposed* to learn as toddlers, playing comfortably while a loving caretaker (male or female) quietly mirrored approval from across the room.

"Alone in the presence of others." Twenty years ago, I used to rely on my dog for this. Now, it's built into my computer screen.

Welcome to the fabulous world of e-mirroring.

Location, Location, Location

As we all know, that computer-animated paper clip isn't going to cut the mustard when we get blocked. We need other ways to tolerate various levels of solitude.

Let's try another parallel monologue to help you select both a public and a private place to write. Remember that the right brain, being dominant for emotion, is more strongly affected by solitude, which at times may engender feelings of loneliness, loss, or isolation. At other times, solitude may provide a welcome relief from the aggravations of everyday life. That is why we need to have both a private and a public place to write.

Try to respond to the following two top ten lists, first with your dominant hand and then with your nondominant hand. Check off as many options as you'd like.

Your Private Writing Site

Dominant Hand
Top Ten Ways to Find Solitude for Writing

___ 1. Write in an office.
___ 2. Write in the bedroom.
___ 3. Write at the dining-room table.
___ 4. Write in your car (parked, of course).
___ 5. Write in study carrel at a library.
___ 6. Write in your writing "nest."
___ 7. Write in your living room.
___ 8. Write in your front yard/on the front porch.
___ 9. Write in your backyard/on the back porch.
___10. Other:_____

Now, switch hands, and respond to this list again. Remember to go with your first impulse.

<u>Nondominant Hand</u>

Top Ten Ways to Find Solitude for Writing

___ 1. Write in an office.

___ 2. Write in the bedroom.

___ 3. Write at the dining-room table.

___ 4. Write in your car (parked, of course).

___ 5. Write in study carrel at a library.

___ 6. Write in your writing "nest."

___ 7. Write in your living room.

___ 8. Write in your front yard/on the front porch.

___ 9. Write in your backyard/on the back porch.

___10. Other:_____

As usual, I had different responses from the two sides of my brain. My nondominant hand checked off numbers 3, 4, 7, and 9, while my dominant hand checked off numbers 1, 4, 5, 6, 7, and 9. Interestingly, my right brain, in choosing the dining-room table, the car, the living room, and the back porch, selected sites where I just might run into other people—so I wouldn't necessarily have to endure too much solitude. On the other hand, my left brain was comfortable with a wider variety of writing sites. In agreement with my right brain, my left brain selected my car, the living room, and the back porch. However, it also showed a preference for writing in my office, a study carrel at a library, and my writing studio—all sites where my solitude would be more or less guaranteed.

These different responses reflect my penchant in the past for avoiding solitude, as well as my current ability to tolerate—and welcome—solitude more often than not. As you examine your answers to this exercise, feel free to utilize a variety of your chosen options so that you can be flexible in responding to the needs of both sides of the brain during any given writing session.

Now let's select some options for your public writing site—for those days when you absolutely cannot tolerate solitude, but still need to write. Again, answer first with your dominant hand, then with your nondominant hand, checking off any items that may apply.

Your Public Writing Site

Dominant Hand
Top Ten Ways to Escape the Loneliness of Solitude— and Still Write

___ 1. Write in a crowded café.

___ 2. Write in a library.

___ 3. Write in a subway.

___ 4. Write on a bus.

___ 5. Write in a park.

___ 6. Write in a diner.

___ 7. Write in a coffee shop.

___ 8. Write in a fast-food restaurant.

___ 9. Write in a bookstore.

___10. Other:_____

Now, check off your responses with your other hand, and see what comes up.

<u>Nondominant Hand</u>
Top Ten Ways to Escape the Loneliness of Solitude— and Still Write

___ 1. Write in a crowded café.
___ 2. Write in a library.
___ 3. Write in a subway.
___ 4. Write on a bus.
___ 5. Write in a park.
___ 6. Write in a diner.
___ 7. Write in a coffee shop.
___ 8. Write in a fast-food restaurant.
___ 9. Write in a bookstore.
___10. Other:_____

No big surprises here for me: As usual, the right and left sides of my brain just can't seem to agree—at least not in full. The right side of my brain checked off numbers 1, 5, 6, and 8, while the left side of my brain checked off numbers 1, 5, 6, 7, 8, 9, and 10.

And I think I know why. The right side of my brain chose places where I would be surrounded by people, but not anyone I know (crowded café, park, diner, fast-food restaurant). My left brain chose these as well, along with two other places where I *might* see someone I know: a coffee shop or a bookstore, traditional magnets for kindred creative spirits everywhere. My left brain also wrote in a response for number 10: an airplane.

These answers reflect the fact that in the past, I would most likely choose a public place where I could be anonymous. However, I have more choices now that I've developed my skills in setting limits with others *("Thanks for stopping by—let's get together next week; I need to get back to my writing")* as well as my ability to shield what I'm writing from other passengers on an airplane. Either way, it's nice to have more choices for my public writing sites.

As you notice your responses to this exercise, try to remember that none of this is absolute. Your preferences may change over time—or even during the course of one day. Feel free to allow yourself as many options as you'd like for your public writing site.

Because you can.

Taking Trigger for a Stroll Down Memory Lane

Now that you have decided on your private and public writing arena, it's important to remember that you want to avoid the natural drift of unconscious entropy. In other words, although your right brain may crave a writing nest that pleases you, the right brain—aka, the unconscious—may at times veer toward what is familiar, whether it's good for you or not. If your desk starts to fill up with clutter again, you may or may not know why, but it's important to resist that impulse toward chaotic living.

Before I knew anything about the importance of setting for my writing, I spent years being ruled by my right brain's all-or-nothing pattern. I vacillated from a stark to a chaotic writing arena. Of course, with my right brain still searching for what's familiar, whether I wrote in a spartan area or one whipped up by a tornado, I was unconsciously re-creating some of the sensory input that was most likely to trigger disquieting memories from the past.

I have worked with many writers who unwittingly set up their writing areas steeped in self-sabotage. For example, I worked with one client who enjoyed bright colors, but her writing studio was comprised of dark, drab colors—reminiscent of the dark household in which she'd been raised. She even had photographs on the desk that were disquieting to her (people who had hurt her in the past). Needless to say, once she had discovered the self-sabotaging nature of her sense of "design," she ditched the photos and made a beeline for the local mall in search of brighter horizons for her studio.

Another client, a biologist and struggling novelist, had set up his writing area on the same desk he'd used to write his doctoral dissertation—complete with piles of papers still glaring at him from four years of research on avian flight patterns! This same client, who had chronic back pain, would sit in an uncomfortable wooden chair, which was situated in a cramped, basement-level room doused with the irritating glare of overhead fluorescent lights—a powerful reminder of his misery in a windowless, fluorescent-dappled grade school, where he'd suffered constant criticism due to his undiagnosed AD/HD. He began to realize that his writing studio was so uncomfortable—both mentally and physically—that he couldn't concentrate there. As a result, he relocated his writing arena to a room with plenty of windows and more natural lighting, traded in the old desk and chair for more ergonomic models, and packed away his dissertation papers in boxes (to be sorted sometime in the next decade or so).

For these clients, and many others, I have recommended various changes in their writing arenas. I usually suggest a desk with shelves for vertical-tiered file holders, a comfortable chair (with lumbar support and "waterfall seating" to support legs and back), and, of course, good lighting. (I also frequently recommend an excellent book called *Organizing for the Creative Person: Right-Brain Styles for Conquering Clutter, Mastering Time, and Reaching Your Goals* by Dorothy Lehmkuhl and Dolores Cotter Lamping.)

Right now, you're probably wondering what inner psychodynamic rip tides may be drawing you away from your own ideal writing nest. Alternatively, you may already know from whence your angst springs. In either case, if you find that you are languishing in a tidal pool of depression or swept into a wave of anxiety at the very sight of your current—or newly designed—writing area, it may be helpful to consult with a licensed mental health professional to find out if your writer's block is being triggered by an unplanned trip down memory lane. (You *can* move forward, and take the fork in the road that's best for you.)

In the next chapter, you'll learn how to get inside your own brain and choose the best mood for your writing time, which may increase the likelihood that you'll actually use the ideal writing sites you have just selected.

See you there.

CHAPTER 5

getting in the mood:

how to overcome
the write-or-flight response

Writers are notorious for using any reason

to keep from working: over-researching,

retyping, going to meetings, waxing the

floors—anything.

—Gloria Steinem

It is my contention that in order to keep a

Muse, you must first offer food.

—Ray Bradbury

Random Acts of Chocolate

"I have to be in the mood to write." So sayeth the would-be writer.

But what exactly is this elusive writing mood—and how do we get it, without resorting to random acts of chocolate?

In order to face the Muse, most writers crave a burst of mental energy. We want all neurons firing and ready for takeoff—no matter that our brains are housed in skulls and are attached to spinal cords, which are attached to those entities called bodies. As writers, we live in our brains. We scurry about like a gaggle of goosenecked Groucho Marxes, our heads forever a good ten inches in front of our bodies. Most of the time, we forget that we're even *in* bodies.

This may work for the occasional writer who has made it past all the hurdles, but for most of us, this will not do. Even the prolific Stephen King, in his book *On Writing*, heralds physical fitness as one of many factors that contribute to good writing.

I've worked with so many writers who, before they could sit down to write, would wait for a tidal wave of energy to wash over them—and, of course, it rarely did, so most of the time they just didn't write.

Take, for example, the case of Jennifer, a stay-at-home mother with four-year-old twins. Although both children were now in preschool, Jennifer still felt that the only time she could concentrate enough to write was after the twins were in bed. On the rare occasions when she tried to surf a wave of creativity, she'd throw herself into a writing frenzy that lasted far too long, resulting in, yes, some good writing, but also a strained back, stiff neck, and a backlog of life maintenance that she'd ignored—activities like eating, sleeping, returning calls. In the same way that children engage in magical thinking, she'd write for hours, as if somehow she could complete a novel in a day. And no matter how much she wrote, it didn't feel like enough.

What's the alternative? For me, in the past, there was none. The thought of doing something—especially writing—a little at a time was not an option for me. My "all-or-nothing" right brain refused to believe that such a piecemeal method of writing could work.

Right about now, though, if you're really blocked, you're probably thinking that "all" part of the all-or-nothing equation doesn't sound so bad. The problem is, doing a batch of "all" means we have to be in a nearly manic state, which works for that day, but not the next. Although we may feel superior to our coworkers who come in late, hung over, or not at all, we can't exactly look an employer in the eye and say, "Sorry I'm late/not focused/unprepared for work today—I have a writing hangover." Somehow, I just can't picture *anyone's* boss saying, "Well that's just great. See you on the bestseller list!"

So how do we learn to balance our need for that elusive writing mood with the fact that we have to keep living the rest of our lives? First, we need to understand *why* we believe this intense mood is necessary. Secondly, we need to learn how to *choose* our moods. Thirdly, we need to choose which *stage* of the six-part writing process our mood-dependent brains can tolerate on a given day. Finally, we need to learn how to use the bi-vocal technique of *interior dialogue* along with a Write-or-Flight Response Chart to make active decisions about when—and what—we'll write.

Got Dopamine?

For many writers, that well-worn path to the refrigerator can be traced directly to our need for that elusive writing mood. Most of us don't go running for carrot sticks, either—it's the Big Three or bust:

1. Sugar
2. Chocolate
3. White flour

And if those don't get our neurons firing, we'll go for one of the Three Cs:

Caffeine
Cigarettes
More chocolate

What do all these substances have in common? They all raise the levels of dopamine and/or serotonin in the brain—two of the critical brain chemicals needed for focus, energy, and concentration. (Epinephrine, endorphins, and other neurotransmitters and hormones are important, too, but we'll stick to dopamine and serotonin for simplicity's sake.) Accordingly, you may be drawn to anything that will increase the levels of these neurotransmitters. (That includes alcohol, marijuana, cocaine, and just about every other possibly addictive/compulsive behavior—even gambling and sex!)

The problem is this: Hershey's, Maxwell House, Marlboros, and the rest of the gang only work in the short-term. Consider once again, for example, the work of Dr. Robert Thayer, who has conducted research by asking hundreds of Psychology 101 students to do things like eat chocolate or go for a five-minute walk (hardly what I got to do for course credit, but hey—why begrudge them the benefits of cutting-edge research?). Results showed that a brisk five-minute walk raises energy levels for 1½ hours. However, after feeding these unsuspecting college students a jolt of dopamine (read: chocolate), Thayer found that their energy levels rose for about one hour—and then plummeted to a subterranean zone below their initial levels. The same is true for caffeine.

In other words, that chocolate doughnut and double mocha java may offer a gust of energy for an hour's worth of writing—which could be all you need on that particular day, give or take a few Winston Lights—but in the long run, you have to consume these substances frequently to keep your creative sails billowing.

And of course, that means although we might sit down to write, our hips no longer fit in that favorite chair, our bodies are shooting out massive amounts of caffeine-induced stress hormones like cortisol (which, according to researchers such as Dr. Pamela Peeke, may increase abdominal fat), and our heart, lungs, and intestines are headed for parts unknown. So what's a writer to do? How can we get the Muse in the mood to write without getting our bodies and brains addled by substances that only help us short-term and manage to hurt us long-term?

One way to cajole the Muse into stopping by on a daily basis is to ask her what mood *she's* in. Let's recall that in Dr. Robert

Thayer's research, he found that we have four basic mood states during the course of a typical day:

1. Tense-tired
2. Tense-energy
3. Calm-energy
4. Calm-tired

Most people careen from *tense-tired* (do-nothing) to *tense-energy* (do-it-all), usually by way of caffeine, nicotine, or sugar. Keeping in mind that the *calm-energy* mood is best for motivation and the *calm-tired* mood is best for evening relaxation so we're well-rested for the next day of productive writing, it's no wonder that the Great American Novel languishes unwritten at the bottom of our unconscious minds.

How do we change all this? As you might guess, the answer is in the right side of the brain. Remember that the right side of the brain controls the biochemistry of our mood states, as well as our reactions to them. For many of us, the right brain was conditioned early on to be a bit off balance when it comes to the optimal levels of dopamine, serotonin, norepinephrine, endorphins, and other mood-altering neurotransmitters and hormones that affect our motivation.

As discussed in Chapter 2, this biochemical quirk, which so many of us have, is created during the first three years of life, when neural pathways are first forming. Researchers, such as Dr. Allan Schore, who study early right-brain development have recently found that this road map for neurotransmitters is crucial to our capacity for concentration, focus, and motivation in later life. For example, the neural pathways for dopamine (which, as adults, we glean from chocolate, caffeine, or protein) are formed by the age of two. By age three, we have formed our neural pathways for serotonin (which, as adults, we siphon from sugar, white flour, and fat) as well as our neural pathways for endorphins (which, as adults, we extract from sugary and high-fat foods).

Let's recall from Chapter 2 how these neural pathways developed.

An infant's brain is programmed to create an attachment with a caregiver to ensure that the baby will be fed, clothed, and sheltered. To create this attachment bond, the delicate balance in the biochemistry of an infant's brain will respond to visual input from caregivers. During infancy, before we can use language, the nonverbal, sensory-oriented right brain is dominant in *everyone*. Researchers such as Dr. Schore have found that whenever the infant's dominant, stimulation-seeking right brain sees love in the caretaker's eyes, that child's right brain will shoot out fireworks of mood-enhancing neurotransmitters like dopamine—precisely what we need in later life for concentration and motivation. Ideally, caregivers will provide the child with appropriate visual stimulation, healthy love, consistent guidance, and emotional reassurance, so the child's neural network will develop normally.

In this ideal scenario, the child develops a healthy balance among the brain chemicals needed in later life for focus and achievement—particularly dopamine, serotonin, and endorphins. Now, I don't know about you, but I didn't exactly grow up on the set of *The Brady Bunch*, so that "healthy balance" wasn't installed in my hard drive.

For most of us, our caregivers were just too busy having a life to gaze lovingly at us for hours at a time—or maybe even at all. Or perhaps our caregivers were too busy filling up their own dopamine or serotonin coffers with food or alcohol or whatever got them through the night. Think about it: What was life like for your parents when you were born? Were they lolling around in *Mister Rogers' Neighborhood*—or were they stressed out from moving halfway across the country, from having three children under the age of five, from financial problems, from a recent death or divorce, from a serious illness, from a miscarriage, from undiagnosed depression, severe PMS, AD/HD, or whatever else life had thrown at them?

In other words, because of the human condition, many of us just didn't get what we needed in terms of a secure attachment—and that means our neural pathways for dopamine and other neurotransmitters might be sketchy in some areas. As a result, as we discussed briefly in Chapter 2, it's clear that many of us display the classic profile that researchers have correlated with insecure attachment styles:

- Extremely high or extremely low levels of arousal in the sympathetic (do-it-all) and parasympathetic (do-nothing) nervous systems
- Negative emotions
- Distracted attention

So, are we doomed to a life of misery and writer's block because Dad got fired and hit the bottle when we were two, and Mom struggled with postpartum depression after having twins, and Grandma died that same year (and don't forget about the effects of World War II or Vietnam)? Of course not.

The bad news: Yes, your parents were having a life like the rest of us, so chances are your dopamine and serotonin pathways have a few detours and dead-ends.

The good news: There are ways to compensate for all that shoddy neural construction.

What we need to do is develop a "secure attachment" style, which, as we discussed in Chapter 2, has been found to be associated with (1) moderate levels of arousal in the sympathetic and parasympathetic nervous systems, (2) positive emotions, and (3) focused attention—in other words, perhaps what Dr. Thayer would call *calm-energy*.

Although we can't exactly summon up the spirit of H. G. Wells and request a quick trip in his time machine to mend the early ways of our parents, we can certainly develop this sense of secure attachment *within ourselves*. We'll do this by getting the right brain to start trusting the more logical, adultlike left brain so the two sides can work as a team, rather than against each other. We'll also teach the left brain how to cajole the right brain in a more calm, compassionate, and competent voice than it usually spews.

Your mission, should you choose to accept it, has four goals:

1. To shape your left brain into a compassionate—not castigating—guide for your right brain

2. To help your childlike right brain develop a "secure attachment style" with your more adultlike and newly enlightened left brain

3. To offer your right brain a continuum of choices between overdrive and comatose

4. To show your visually-oriented right brain these choices in an easy-to-use chart

By using these approaches, you can short-circuit the right brain's attempts at self-sabotage—and, in so doing, allow your writing energy to flow.

Choosing Your Mood

In previous chapters, by accessing the voices of both your left and right brain, you've learned how to give yourself permission to write, how to create a comfortable writing process, how to make time to write, and how to choose several places to write. Now, we can use this same bi-vocal process to get you in the mood to write.

As you can see from the Mood-Choice Charts that follow, the all-or-nothing right brain thinks in terms of comatose and overdrive, and it needs to be shown that there are gradations between these two extremes. Research shows that these two extremes are not the best states of mind for task completion.

As you may recall from Chapter 2, the right side of the brain controls the sympathetic nervous system and its fight-or-flight response patterns. If the sympathetic nervous system is overly aroused, we are too *anxious* to get anything done. Of course, if the parasympathetic nervous system is overly aroused, we are too *apathetic* to get anything done. The left brain knows all this, but it usually has a hard time convincing the right brain—capricious ruler of that not-so-sympathetic nervous system—that going to extremes will get us nowhere.

And remember, for those of us who were raised under conditions of chronic or severe stress, (1) the right and left sides of the brain are not as well integrated, so we need to work harder to make the two sides of the brain cooperate, and (2) our hippocampus is likely to be smaller, so we have more trouble managing the fight-or-flight response. In order to change all this—so we'll write rather than take flight—the left brain needs to establish a more "secure attachment" with the right brain by approaching it in an age-appropriate manner. Remember that the right brain, which is dominant until age three, responds like a toddler, so we need to offer options that are *concrete and specific*. We need to explain what *to do*, rather than what *not to do*. For example, telling a restaurant-resistant toddler "Don't stand on the table" is a lot less effective than saying, "We need to keep our feet on the floor."

In offering concrete, specific choices, the left brain must also appeal to the visual dominance of the right brain. For example, telling a toddler "Don't leave the yard" isn't as effective as putting up a picket fence and saying, "Stay in front of the white sticks." Seeing is believing, but seeing is also understanding when it comes to the highly visual right brain.

In the same way, when we're trying to write, spelling it out for the right brain can help. To say, "Don't go to extremes" is not concrete or specific. What the right brain needs to hear is a clear voice that says, "Here are some easy choices you can make to balance your mood state" or "Pick the number you like on the chart."

Simply telling the perpetually immature right brain all the logical reasons for balancing out your mood state won't get you very far. In the world of parenting skills, according to experts such as Dr. Thomas Phelan, there is a myth called "the little adult assumption," which means that we mistakenly assume that children are just miniature versions of adults. We want to believe that if we explain something often enough, at some point the kid will say, "Oh, I see why you want me to do that, and now that I understand, I'll be happy to do that."

Not going to happen. The reality is that children are not miniature adults. Their systems of logical thinking are not fully developed, and this will always be true of the right brain, whose motto is, "It's never too late to have an eternal childhood." In other words, when the left brain says, *"Just do it,"* the right brain, like any two-year-old, stamps its foot and says, *"No."*

Let's take a moment to see how this works. Think of a small writing task you'd like to complete: perhaps editing a letter, outlining an article, or writing a page of dialogue.

Then, allow your left brain to present the following Mood Choice Charts to your right brain. First, use your nondominant hand to check off your current level of energy and tension by placing an *X* near the number that best represents your current mood.

Then, still using your nondominant hand, mark the next box for the level of energy and tension you feel you *need* right now to do this task.

Nondominant Hand
Current Level of Focus:

Comatose................................. Overdrive
0 1 2 3 4 5 6 7 8 9 10

Desired Level of Focus:

Comatose................................. Overdrive
0 1 2 3 4 5 6 7 8 9 10

Now, do the same two exercises, only this time, use your dominant hand to mark the boxes that apply to your current motivational state, and then your desired motivational state.

Dominant Hand
Current Level of Focus:

Comatose................................. Overdrive
0 1 2 3 4 5 6 7 8 9 10

Desired Level of Focus:

Comatose................................. Overdrive
0 1 2 3 4 5 6 7 8 9 10

Do you notice any differences in the expectations and needs expressed by your nondominant versus your dominant hand?

When I did this exercise just now while writing this chapter, the results surprised me. With my nondominant hand, I felt like I was nearly comatose (1), and that I needed to be in overdrive (8 to 10) to get this chapter done. However, when I answered with my dominant hand, I marked my current energy level as 3, and felt I needed to attain an energy level of 6 to get this done. As you can see, my right brain (as represented by my nondominant left hand) is truly steeped in all-or-nothing dogma, but my more logical, adultlike left brain (as represented by my dominant right hand) can tell that I'm alert enough to type this, but could still use a boost to continue writing if I'm going to go on much longer today.

Somewhere between the two sides of my brain, I need to find a compromise. If I'm going to continue writing today, I need to make sure I have the mental energy to do so. I've chosen my mood—I'll go with that 6 suggested by my dominant brain—but how am I going to get it?

The Art of Mood-Shaping: Ben & Jerry Meet the Dalai Lama

Think of your favorite writer. Is he or she fondly portrayed as moody, neurotic, chain-smoking, binge-drinking, or perhaps "eccentric"? Isn't that part of being a writer?

We have to be a bit quirky to be writers in the first place, but the irony is that such quirkiness or moodiness can make it *impossible* to write. We envision ourselves as brilliant, creative spirits burning the midnight oil with buckets of Starbucks and cartons of Marlboros—sacrificing time, energy, and even our health for the cause.

This may work to get some writers in the mood, but recent research proves that we now have choices that were unavailable or unknown in the past. Although we may yearn for that romantic image of the toiling writer alone with the stars and the Muse, it's probably better to choose healthier—and more reliable—ways to blast our brains into the galaxy of creativity. Certainly, Dorothy Parker and Ernest Hemingway were brilliant writers—but look what happened to them.

We all know that sufficient sleep, balanced nutrition, and regular exercise will prime our brains for optimal writing—but that doesn't mean we're going to live that way. Instead, we choose faster, but less efficient, ways to increase our motivation.

Let's see which side of the brain is choosing these options. Following is another parallel monologue exercise. Respond as quickly as possible, checking off any items that appeal to you—first with your dominant hand, and then with your nondominant hand.

Dominant Hand
Top Ten Traditional Ways to Blast Your Brain into Writing Mode

___10. Caffeine—coffee or tea

___ 9. Caffeine—cola

___ 8. Chocolate—any form

___ 7. Cigarettes

___ 6. Candy

___ 5. Cookies

___ 4. Ice cream

___ 3. Salty snacks—potato chips, Fritos, pretzels, etc.

___ 2. Alcohol or other drugs

___ 1. Staying up late

Now, let's see what the other side of your brain has to say. Again, choose quickly, using your nondominant hand to mark any item that appeals to you.

Nondominant Hand
Top Ten Traditional Ways to Blast Your Brain into Writing Mode

___10. Caffeine—coffee or tea

___ 9. Caffeine—cola

___ 8. Chocolate—any form

___ 7. Cigarettes

___ 6. Candy

___ 5. Cookies

___ 4. Ice cream

___ 3. Salty snacks—potato chips, Fritos, pretzels, etc.

___ 2. Alcohol or other drugs

___ 1. Staying up late

Surprise, surprise. As usual, in my case, the right hand still doesn't know what the left hand is doing.

When I responded to this exercise, my dominant hand checked off numbers 10, 9, 8, and 3: coffee/tea, cola, chocolate, and salty snacks. However, the other side of my brain definitely wanted more options—the less healthy, the better. It checked off numbers 9, 8, 7, 6, 5, 4, 3, and 1: cola, chocolate, cigarettes, candy, cookies, ice cream, salty snacks, and staying up late—just about anything a rebellious child, or teenager, might want. Not surprisingly, the only two that my nondominant brain *didn't* choose were those traditionally reserved for grownups: coffee/tea and alcohol/drugs.

If your responses to this exercise reveal a discrepancy between the two sides of your brain, notice which set of options you usually choose, as opposed to which ones *you wish you'd choose*. But before we decide which side of our brain will be in charge of our writing moods, we might wonder if there are other options that researchers like Dr. Robert Thayer have discovered for creating the ideal motivational state of calm-energy.

Let us count the ways.

Top Ten Research-Based Ways to Create Calm-Energy

___10. Adequate amount of sleep (between seven and nine hours per night)

___ 9. Taking a twenty- to thirty-minute nap sometime between noon and 4 P.M.

___ 8. Taking a brisk five-minute walk

___ 7. Eating a healthy, well-balanced diet

- *Avoid*: white flour products, sugar, diet colas with aspartame, alcohol/drugs
- *Eat more:*
    - Complex carbohydrates (fruits, vegetables, whole grains)
    - Lean proteins (for more energy, eat three ounces of protein *before* eating carbohydrates)
- *Drink more:*
    - Herbal teas to relax (chamomile, rosemary)
    - Green teas for mental alertness (avoid edgy physical energy from coffee)

___ 6. Exercise (especially yoga)

___ 5. Sitting in a warm (not hot) bath (no more than 103 degrees)

___ 4. Sitting in a Jacuzzi for no more than ten minutes

___ 3. Meditation

___ 2. Massage

___ 1. Writing/conversing/laughing about your stress

Well, you're probably thinking, forget number 6 and number 7—and 10 is impossible right now, but, hey, that nap sounds like a good idea.

So, before you leave the office for a night of writing, you can tell your boss that after you have your afternoon nap, you'll take a brisk five-minute walk to your car when you leave early to get a massage, followed by a stint in a Jacuzzi at the gym while you eat a baked potato with cottage cheese instead of sour cream, and you promise that while you drive home in the lotus position you'll hum *Om. . .*

for his soul and yours until you come back to work tomorrow—late, of course, since you need your biochemical beauty sleep.

Okay, so nobody works for the Dalai Lama. You can't afford to lose your day job—or the respect of your family and friends.

But maybe some of these remedies are possible. Let's peruse a few ideas that may make these energy-boosting strategies more appealing—and your writing time more productive.

First of all, perhaps number 10 is good idea: Research indicates that people who don't get adequate amounts of sleep (seven to nine hours per night) have 20 percent less mood-enhancing serotonin and are more likely to become depressed. (Chronic insomniacs are forty times more likely to become depressed.) And what's the first thing to fly out the window if you're even *mildly* depressed? Motivation—and she takes her best friend, Concentration, with her.

Chronic sleep deprivation also triggers an excess of the stress hormone cortisol, which in turn will eventually create a *tense-tired* mood, as well as cravings for high-fat foods, which can slow down cognitive processing: Hello, brain sludge; goodbye Great American Novel.

So, am I saying that sleeping more will improve your chances of writing? *Yes.*

Am I saying that we should reject our favorite foods and jog five miles a day? *No.*

Balancing our mood states can be a challenge. We all know that exercise will give us more energy, but how do we crawl our way to the gym in the first place? Instead, the right brain has us wolfing down our usual sugar-soaked and caffeine-laden "mood-elevators"—which take us to the bottom floor and leave us there.

But even if you can't see yourself popping broccoli tops on your lunch hour, you can still *choose your moods* by combining your usual methods with new strategies.

For example, chocolate lovers have a difficult time giving up their daily dose of comfort food—they don't call them Hershey's *Kisses* for nothing. Now, there's nothing wrong with eating chocolate: No doubt many an M&M has contributed to many writers' creative output. As a matter of fact, in *Eating Well for Optimum Health,* Dr. Andrew Weil suggests that if you're going to eat chocolate, dive into dark chocolate. Unlike milk chocolate, dark chocolate contains the "good" monounsaturated fat found in olive oil, so you might as well be healthy while you're scarfing down those Godiva chocolates.

In other words, we don't have to let the right brain's all-or-nothing style dictate the way we create our writing moods; we don't have to go into total deprivation mode and live on alfalfa sprouts and tofu. For example, if you're going to eat chocolate, why not try a cup of green tea with it? Although some chocolate products actually release more energy-raising dopamine than coffee, green tea not only raises your energy level for much longer than the one hour you'll get from chocolate or coffee, but it also gives you more mental alertness, without the edginess. And, unlike chocolate, coffee, or black tea, green tea will not boomerang you back to a "tense-tired" mood an hour after ingestion. (Green tea also helps to regulate your body's insulin levels to promote weight loss—so you needn't worry when the camera adds ten pounds for your *Booknotes* interview on C-SPAN!)

As noted in the previous top ten list, other ways to increase mental energy for writing include taking a brisk five-minute walk (research shows a marked rise in energy for 1½ hours afterward), eating frequent small meals that start with three ounces of protein (to keep the brain stoked with dopamine), taking a twenty- to thirty-minute nap between noon and 4 P.M. (to avoid disrupting circadian rhythms), doing yoga or meditation (both increase serotonin), or using mood-altering herbal remedies. For example, ginkgo is said to increase mental alertness, while ginseng, ginger, and garlic can increase physical energy. And, direct from the honeycomb: bee pollen, bee propolis, and royal jelly also raise energy levels that may help you focus on writing.

On the other hand, if you're stuck in a *tense-energy* mood and need to calm down enough to be able to focus on your writing, other herbal remedies can help reduce tension: lobelia, valerian root, lavender, and chamomile to name a few. Aromatherapy can also be helpful in alleviating tension (lavender oil), as well as raising energy (peppermint oil).

However, it's important to remember that many modern-day medicines are derived from plants and herbs, so using herbal remedies—especially in conjunction with psychotropic medication—can be dangerous if you have not consulted with a medical professional or a naturopathic physician. For a good overview, peruse Mark Mayell's book *Natural Energy* or James and Phyllis Balch's *Prescription for Nutritional Healing*. Michael Norden's book, *Beyond Prozac*, is also a helpful resource for natural ways to raise energy and lower tension, especially through food choices.

For example, according to experts such as Dirk Pearson, eating three ounces of dopamine-releasing protein a few minutes before you eat any serotonin-releasing carbohydrates will create a stronger surge of energy than you'd get if you ate the protein along with the carbohydrates. In the race to rush through the brain, calming serotonin will always win over energizing dopamine. Translation: Keep a handful of unshelled peanuts in your writing studio at all times! They take longer to consume than shelled peanuts, and crushing those shells can be a great way to release tension while you pop those dollops of protein. *Then*—if you still want to—go for that Häagen-Dazs.

The idea here is to start adding in elements to your life before you subtract anything, because the childlike right brain can so easily feel deprived—and that's what gets us into this mess in the first place! Don't throw out the chocolate with the bath water: Make a pitcher of iced green tea—sans sugar—and keep it on hand to mix and match with those M&M's.

Believe it or not, right now, while I'm writing this chapter, I have on my desk a glass of iced green tea and a glass of ice water—and I do go back and forth. My right brain, like yours, loves to revel in having *choices*. (The water, by the way, is great for keeping back and neck muscles hydrated, which prevents rigor mortis by the end of any given writing session.) When I offer my writing clients these and other energy-raising options, I notice that they tend to pick the following most often. See which ones you choose—first with your dominant hand, then with your nondominant hand.

Dominant Hand

**Top Ten Frequently Chosen *New* Ways to
Get in the Mood to Write**

___10. Hot or iced green tea

___ 9. Hot or iced green tea with a dark chocolate bar

___ 8. Hot or iced green tea with a handful of mixed nuts

___ 7. Black tea with trail mix

___ 6. Brisk five-minute walk

___ 5. Twenty rapid deep breaths (don't tell anyone, but this is yoga)

___ 4. Small meals with protein (chicken, cottage cheese, nuts)

___ 3. Twenty-minute nap (between noon and 4 P.M.)

___ 2. Black tea (hot or iced) with cheese and crackers

___ 1. Herbal capsules of ginger, garlic, ginseng, or ginkgo

Now, switch hands so you can see what the other half of your brain may want to try the next time you sit down to write.

Nondominant Hand

**Top Ten Frequently Chosen *New* Ways to
Get in the Mood to Write**

___10. Hot or iced green tea

___ 9. Hot or iced green tea with a dark chocolate bar

___ 8. Hot or iced green tea with a handful of mixed nuts

___ 7. Black tea with trail mix

___ 6. Brisk five-minute walk

___ 5. Twenty rapid deep breaths (don't tell anyone, but this is yoga)

___ 4. Small meals with protein (chicken, cottage cheese, nuts)

___ 3. Twenty-minute nap (between noon and 4 P.M.)

___ 2. Black tea (hot or iced) with cheese and crackers

___ 1. Herbal capsules of ginger, garlic, ginseng, or ginkgo

Today, when I did this parallel monologue, my dominant hand chose numbers 10, 6, 5, 4, 2, and 1. My nondominant hand, however, chose numbers 10, 9, 4, 3, and 2. Apparently, both sides of my brain like iced green tea, small protein-packed meals, and cups of black tea. But only my left brain will go for five-minute walks, twenty rapid deep breaths, or herbal capsules for energy. My right brain, however, is more than happy to grab a dark chocolate bar to go with that iced green tea and to sneak in a twenty-minute nap between noon and 4 P.M. On any given day, I may engage in some or all of these energy-boosting strategies—the point is to choose them consciously.

Of course, just because my clients want to try these new energy-boosters doesn't mean they'll swear off Pepsi and Doritos for life. The idea here is simply to make conscious choices about how you create your writing moods rather than allowing your right brain to catapult you to the nearest Starbucks as a way to *avoid* writing.

Let's see how we can convince your right brain that, when it comes to getting in the mood to write, there's more to life than Milky Ways and iced cappuccino. Think of another small writing task you'd like to accomplish: reading an article for your dissertation, editing two pages of a manuscript, typing a few footnotes, or perhaps brainstorming a title for a story.

Now, let's go back to our Mood Choice Charts. Mark an *X* near the number that best represents your current mood, and then your desired mood. Do the exercise twice—first with your nondominant hand, and then with your dominant hand.

Nondominant Hand
Current Level of Focus:

Comatose................................ Overdrive

0 1 2 3 4 5 6 7 8 9 10

Desired Level of Focus:

Comatose................................ Overdrive

0 1 2 3 4 5 6 7 8 9 10

Now, do the same two exercises, only this time, use your dominant hand to mark the boxes that apply to your current motivational state, and then your desired motivational state.

Dominant Hand
Current Level of Focus:

Comatose................................ Overdrive

0 1 2 3 4 5 6 7 8 9 10

Desired Level of Focus:

Comatose................................ Overdrive

0 1 2 3 4 5 6 7 8 9 10

Again, notice if there are any differences—or similarities—in your responses to these exercises. Based on both sides of your brain, decide whether you need to move from tense-tired (or calm-tired) to tense-energy (or calm-energy).

Now that you've chosen your mood, let's decide how you'd like to create it. By using the following menu of Mood-Shaping Choices, you can raise energy, lower tension, or both. (Some of the choices are listed in all three categories, so you may just want to pick one of them for general use.)

- If you need *more energy* (perhaps you need to move from a 0 to a 5), then select an option from Column A (Increase Energy).
- If you need to feel *more calm* (perhaps you need to move from a 9 to a 5), then select an option from Column B (Decrease Tension).
- If you need to *jettison yourself out of a tense-tired mood*, choose an option from Column C (More Energy + Less Tension), or select one option from Column A and one from Column B.

Top Ten Mood-Shaping Choices

A	B	C
Increase Energy	**Decrease Tension**	**More Energy + Less Tension**
5-minute brisk walk (1½ hours energy)	5-minute brisk walk (1½ hours energy)	5-minute brisk walk (1½ hours energy)
1 yoga stretch	1 yoga stretch	1 yoga stretch
20 rapid, deep breaths	20 slow, deep breaths	20 deep breaths
5-minute meditation (count 1–10 repeatedly)	5-minute meditation (count 1–10 repeatedly)	5-minute meditation (count 1–10 repeatedly)
3 oz. protein (5 min. before carbohydrate)	Complex carbohydrate (fruits, vegetables, whole grains)	Protein + carbohydrate
Herbal capsules: ginkgo, ginger, garlic, ginseng, bee pollen	Herbal capsules: kava, lobelia, valerian root, lavendar	Herbal capsules: sarsaparilla, etc. (see Prescription for Nutritional Healing by J. and P. Balch)
Ginger tea, ginseng tea	Chamomile tea, rosemary tea	Combination herbal teas
20-minute nap (between noon and 4 P.M.)	20-minute nap (between noon and 4 P.M.)	20-minute nap (between noon and 4 P.M.)
10 minutes of exercise	10 minutes of exercise	10 minutes of exercise
Caffeine/chocolate (*green tea =mental focus; *coffee/tea/chocolate = 1 hour physical/mental energy)	Writing about stress	Talking/laughing with a friend

Remember: These are choices, not commands. Pick one that you'd like to try, and start there. Even one small change can make a difference in your mood state, and whether the Muse will stop by—or not.

Now that you've chosen your mood and your method for creating it, you can combine these choices with the task-sprinting option we used in Chapter 2.

And don't forget to use your dopamine-craving right brain rewards from the lists in Chapter 2 to give yourself credit for time served!

Task-Sprinting
Task:_____

Nondominant Hand
             Comatose................................. Overdrive
Current Mood: 0 1 2 3 4 5 6 7 8 9 10
Desired Mood: 0 1 2 3 4 5 6 7 8 9 10

Dominant Hand
             Comatose................................. Overdrive
Current Mood: 0 1 2 3 4 5 6 7 8 9 10
Desired Mood: 0 1 2 3 4 5 6 7 8 9 10

Today, I think I'll choose the energy level selected by my
    ___nondominant brain
    ___dominant brain

To Change Mood: raise energy by ___lower tension by ___

I'll try task for:

__ 2 min. __ 5 min. __ 10 min. __ 15 min. __ 20 min. __ 30 min.

Actual time:

__ 2 min. __ 5 min. __ 10 min. __ 15 min. __ 20 min. __ 30 min.

Reward time:

__ 2 min. __ 5 min. __ 10 min. __ 15 min. __ 20 min. __ 30 min.

By using this chart whenever you want to write, you are actively engaging both sides of the brain—and making conscious decisions about your writing process, instead of letting the day whiz by in a blur of activity that has nothing to do with writing.

The Writer's Choices:
The Six Stages of Writing

The next challenge in using the writing time you selected in Chapter 3 involves choosing which part of the writing process you can tolerate at any given moment.

For example, some mornings, when I have my precious writing time set aside, I am riddled with that familiar tense-tired mood and can't even think about writing a line of dialogue that wouldn't sound like I yanked it from the fugue state I'm wallowing in.

Instead, I'll go through a portion of something I've already written, circle all the adjectives and adverbs—which I know must die so that stronger nouns and verbs may live—and then browse through J. I. Rodale's marvelous book *The Synonym Finder*, looking for replacements. I'll start to remember how much I love words, and often my enthusiasm for writing wells up. I may not write any new sentences, but I sure get my diction spiced up on five or ten pages. Either way, I'm engaged in the *process* of writing.

Think about it: It all has to be done sometime. If it's going to take twenty hours to complete a writing task, it could look like this:

> 1 hour—prewriting (scrawling ideas, outlining, gathering quotations)
> 18 hours—writing (creating sentences)
> 1 hour—rewriting (editing the draft)

Or like this:

> 5 hours—prewriting
> 5 hours—writing
> 10 hours—rewriting

Or like this:

> 12 hours—prewriting
> 2 hours—writing
> 6 hours—rewriting

Every writer is different, and so is every writing project. For example, some tasks will demand more time in the prewriting phase—which usually means we start wailing, "I've been at this for twelve hours, and I haven't even started writing yet!"

Not true. You have started to engage in the *process of writing*—and writing sentences is only one phase of that process. So, on any given day at any given time, depending on the mood you're in, you can usually find at least one part of the writing process you can manage to tackle.

Following is a list of what I call the Writer's Choices. I've taken the liberty of including a few steps beyond the usual prewrite/write/rewrite routine, because these other activities are valid steps in the writing process—so we might as well acknowledge them and give ourselves credit for time served. Some of these are more right-brain processes, while others are more left-brain processes. In selecting which part of the writing process you'll try, you are actively cooperating with your two-sided brain.

The Writer's Choices

I'll choose whichever one of the six stages of writing I can tolerate right now:

___**Read-writing** (reading stories/essays/novels/dissertations similar to my current work; reading what I've already written)

___**Cowriting** (calling other writers to gauge their response to what I've written so far)

___**Rote writing** (typing notes, typing handwritten text, transcribing interviewees' comments, typing up addresses of agents or publishers—anything that requires brain concentration just above a flat line)

___**Prewriting** (jotting down thoughts or creating an outline—making a big mess)

___**Writing** (creating sentences, lines of poetry)

___**Rewriting** (editing: spell-checking, deleting most adjectives/adverbs, intensifying diction by looking up synonyms, polishing sentences, etc.)

Ask yourself which one of these six stages of writing you could do right now. Then, think of any small writing task you'd like to work on, and include it in the following Task-Sprinting Chart.

Task-Sprinting

Stage of writing task I can manage right now:

___read-writing___prewriting___cowriting___writing___rote-writing___rewriting

Particular task/project I can approach right now:_____

Nondominant Hand

Comatose................................. Overdrive

Current Mood: 0 1 2 3 4 5 6 7 8 9 10

Desired Mood: 0 1 2 3 4 5 6 7 8 9 10

Dominant Hand

Comatose................................. Overdrive

Current Mood: 0 1 2 3 4 5 6 7 8 9 10

Desired Mood: 0 1 2 3 4 5 6 7 8 9 10

Today, I think I'll choose the energy level selected by: my
___nondominant brain   ___dominant brain

To Change Mood: *raise energy by___lower tension by___*
I'll try task for:

__ 2 min. __ 5 min. __ 10 min. __ 15 min. __ 20 min. __ 30 min.
Actual time:

__ 2 min. __ 5 min. __ 10 min. __ 15 min. __ 20 min. __ 30 min.
Reward time:

__ 2 min. __ 5 min. __ 10 min. __ 15 min. __ 20 min. __ 30 min.

As you can see, this chart taps into both sides of your brain to launch you into the writing process. See what happens, right now, when you try to follow the task-sprinting plan you just designed.

If you're still stuck, proceed to the next section, where we'll use another whole-brain technique for boosting your motivation to write.

Interior Dialogue: Why Two Heads Are Better Than One

In my work with clients, and in my own struggles with the writing process, I've noticed that sometimes we need more than visual choices to activate the right brain. At these times, we need to appeal directly to the right brain in terms of its dominance for emotional elements that block creativity. In writing fiction, we know how to reveal our characters' inner musings through interior monologue. In this next bi-vocal brain approach, we'll learn how to access our own inner musings by using what I call *interior dialogue.*

If we recall that the right brain is only about three years old at best, then it stands to reason that sometimes the right brain may harbor irrational fears or beliefs, just as any toddler would. These beliefs, not surprisingly, usually revolve around not getting our needs met. The trick is to find out what the right brain wants that it isn't getting—and then find a way to provide it.

When it comes to managing that craving right brain, remember: *Don't deny it; supply it.* Otherwise, that childlike right brain will just grab the time back anyway and sabotage our writing efforts with untold numbers of e-mails, phone calls, caffeine binges, or downright napping.

I use interior dialogue whenever I can't get myself to sit down and write. Once, when my left brain asked, "What's wrong," my right brain responded by saying that it felt "too alone" and needed "more fun." What it wanted, on that particular day, was to call up a fellow writer–friend to go see a movie after writing. My left brain responded by saying "Okay," but that wasn't enough. My right brain actually had the audacity to ask for a promise as to *which movie* I'd see (as my reward for putting in my writing time)—and *what time* I'd see it that day. Although I was unnerved by the intensity of my right brain's demands, I actually went downstairs, checked the newspaper for viewing times, and told to my right brain that I'd go to the 2:10 showing of *Shakespeare in Love.* It was then, and only then, that I could sit down to write.

As a therapist, I knew which questions to ask. I got the answers I needed, acted on them, and was able to write for several hours uninterrupted. I did go to the movie at the promised hour—and enjoyed every minute of it!

Following is a simple script—with pertinent questions—that you can follow whenever you get stuck in your writing process. (Of course, you'll also find a to-go order of this in the appendices.)

Interior Dialogue

Dominant hand: What do you need right now?

Nondominant hand:___

Dominant hand: What would you need to be able to do this writing task?

Nondominant hand:___

Dominant hand: Let me see if I can find a way to get you what you need. Maybe we can___, or we could___, either now or after twenty minutes of writing. Would that help?

Nondominant hand:___

Dominant hand: Okay, then, are you ready to try this for a few minutes?

Nondominant hand:___

If these questions do not appeal to you, following is a list of further questions with slightly different phrasing. *Notice which ones you're drawn to.*

Use your dominant hand to write them down, allowing plenty of space for your nondominant hand to answer back—because it will.

Extended Interior Dialogue

1. What's wrong?   _____
2. How are you feeling?   _____
3. What else are you feeling?   _____
4. What do you think about that?   _____
5. What do you need right now?   _____

6. What do you want right now? _____

7. What else do you want right now? _____

8. What do you need to be able to complete this subtask? _____

9. What would it mean if you did this subtask? _____

10. Tell me more about that. _____

11. What will you need after you complete the subtask? _____

12. What would you like to have after you complete the subtask? _____

13. What would you like to do after you complete the subtask? _____

14. What do you need to have as a reward for doing this? _____

15. What would you like to have as a reward for doing this? _____

16. Which part of the writing process do you feel like doing right now? _____

17. Which writing project do you feel like working on right now? _____

18. Which kind of mood are you in right now—and how can we change it? _____

19. How many minutes would you like to try writing today? _____

20. How many minutes of reward time do you need if you write today? _____

By allowing your newly enlightened left brain to ask compassionate, specific, pertinent questions, you are giving your right brain what it needs: empathy, choices, and guidance.

Yes, it can be unnerving knowing that the two sides of our brains operate so autonomously—but they do, and the sooner we use this to our advantage, the sooner we'll get to our writing. Although interior dialogue may not be the kind of dialogue you'll use in your first novel, you may need to write this kind of dialogue to be *able* to write that first novel.

Voice Lessons: Your "To-Go" Order of Instant Motivation

Now that you've mastered these techniques for cajoling your right brain into letting you write, what do you do when you're facing the blank page alone on a Saturday night—at home or at Starbucks?

Voilà: Here are your voice lessons, aka, choice lessons. Whenever your right brain rears its gnarly little head, the following Write-or-Flight Chart will remind you that writing—or not—is a choice.

Just as you have two voices—the left brain's voice of reason, and the right brain's all-or-nothing voice of panic—you also have two choices: write or flight. If we only listen to the right side of the brain, we'll usually choose the "flight" option, which I call the *half-brained approach.* Our other choice is to listen to both sides of the brain—by using the bi-vocal methods presented in this book—which means we'll choose the option of writing via the *whole-brain approach.*

Keeping in mind the fact that the right brain needs a visual reminder, and that it responds well to humor, the chart provides both. And, because I know you're not going to glue this book to your laptop, you'll find a copy of this chart in Appendix 5, so you'll always have a "to-go" order you can clip as a reminder of the choices you have every day.

For example, as the chart illustrates and as I've mentioned before, it's fine to use what I call the *patchwork quilt method* of writing a novel: Just pick any scene that you think might show up in your novel, and start it. After you've written a number of separate scenes, you'll start to see how they might fit together, a plot line will evolve more readily, and before you know it, your novel is patched together and ready for its first revision.

The following example illustrates the notion that following the right brain's intuition—*which scene do you feel like writing today*—is often the best place to start. Not everyone writes chronologically, or with computer programs at hand, or with a detailed or even a rough outline before they start creating scenes. We are told to start our novels *in medias res*—smack in the middle of things—so why not write them that way, too? If rigid structure and strict chronology haven't worked for you thus far, it may mean your right brain wants first dibs on this story you have to tell—which is not a problem, because the oh-so-logical left brain will help you fit together the patchwork pieces later.

Write-or-Flight Chart

	Flight	Write
Choices	**Half-Brained Approach**	**Whole-Brain Approach**
Goal	*Write novel*	Write a chapter—any chapter
Subgoal	*Do it all*	Write one scene—any scene
Subtask	*What's that?*	Spend 20 minutes writing dialogue (or exposition about the setting) for any scene
Date	*Never*	Tuesday, 2:00–2:20
Reward	Only kick self while down 10 times instead of 30 times	20 minutes of reward time (reading, phone calls, checking e-mail, time toward going to a movie)
Current mood	Tense-tired	Tense-tired
Desired mood	Tense-energy	Calm-energy
Raise energy	Fry brains with coffee; solidify blood with nicotine; coagulate arteries with box of chocolates	Cup of green tea with dark chocolate bar; 5-min. brisk walk (indoors or outdoors); 20 rapid, deep breaths
Reduce tension	Inhale can of Pringles; hook up IV of Häagen-Dazs; scarf down pizza with a beer chaser	Cup of chamomile tea; 5 shoulder scrunches; 20 slow, deep breaths

You get the picture. Whenever I use this chart to jump-start the Muse, I'm reminded that procrastination feels like an unconscious nondecision: We may resolve to write, but the day whizzes by, and once again we haven't done a thing. Instead, this Write-or-Flight Chart helps us to make conscious decisions about writing—or not. It gives your right brain—master of the flight mode—just what it needs to switch over to the writing mode: a bit of humor, and a choice of behaviors you can change *today*.

A Word to the Tense and Tired Writer

Whenever I think about all the lifestyle changes I've recommended to clients over the years, I'm reminded of the first time I read this line in Andrew Weil's book *Eating Well for Optimum Health*, as he described the effects of simple carbohydrates like French fries and Twinkies: "High-glycemic-index foods provide bursts of energy that may be followed quickly by depletions and hunger."

Well, that about sums it up.

What a perfect setup for the all-or-nothing right brain's MO of rollicking between overdrive and comatose. Although I've had some difficulty convincing writers to learn how to do meditation (aka, "the most boring activity possible") and yoga (aka, "the second most boring activity possible"), somewhere in there, with the techniques I've presented in this book, I convinced many of them that a twenty-four-hour roller coaster ride was not the best way to manage the writing process.

On the other hand, do you honestly think I wrote this entire book on nine hours of nightly sleep, sipping delicate green tea, doing countless hours of yoga and meditation—with absolutely no input from Ben & Jerry? Well, guess again. Of course, I *tried* to get enough sleep most days, I did have iced green tea along with far too many Diet Cokes, and I did do yoga, meditation, and plenty of five-minute walks—but not without the requisite input from Ben & Jerry.

But even with those imperfections, as long as I followed the basic path of choosing my moods, I got the job done.

The proof is in your hands.

PART II

daring to write
the bi-vocal way

CHAPTER 6

starting to write:

remembrances of things past

I write any sort of rubbish
which will cover the main outlines of the
story, then I can begin to see it.

—Frank O'Connor

I don't plot,
I just show up at the keyboard every day
to see what's happening.

—Elizabeth Berg

Art is the only thing that can go on
mattering once it has stopped hurting.

—Elizabeth Bowen

"Waiting for Godot"

As a writer, you may avoid the blank page for a number of reasons that rise like gossamer smoke from the past: previous rejections from agents or publishers; negative or lukewarm evaluations from teachers, colleagues, or parents; even life events that at first glance appear unrelated to your identity as a writer. This avoidance may be especially challenging when you try to start new writing projects. You may sit for what seems like an eternity, waiting for that creative flow, but you may as well be waiting for old no-show Godot.

In this chapter, you'll learn how to (1) discern the underlying saboteurs of your creative blockage, and (2) apply the bi-vocal approach to conquer these insidious traitors so they no longer hold you hostage. You'll be able to explore the thoughts and feelings that resonate in the right side of the brain when you ask yourself these three questions:

> Why am I so reluctant to call myself a writer?
> Why can't I begin to write?
> How do I begin to write?

Let Us Count the Ways

For so many of my clients struggling with writer's block, the worst part has been starting a project. The easy part, of course, is conjuring up an Excuse for the Day. There are so many ways that the right brain can sabotage the creative spirit. I'm sure you have your own litany of avoidance methods—with excuses to match—when it comes time to write.

Let's see what pops up when you respond to the following parallel monologue, first with your dominant hand, then with your nondominant hand.

Dominant Hand
When I think of starting a writing task, I feel:_____.

Nondominant Hand
When I think of starting a writing task, I feel:_____.

Check your responses to see how divergent they may be. As usual, my answers weren't the same. When I responded to this exercise today, I wrote "frustrated" with my dominant hand. This is a fairly accurate reading of my mood today, because I am not in the mood to write, nor am I feeling particularly articulate today. (Fortunately, you'll be reading the revised version of this chapter!)

However, when I switched to my nondominant hand, I wrote "scared and nervous." These adjectives accurately portray my right brain's reticence when it comes to writing. Those words also reflect the way I frequently felt as a child—and it's the more childlike, creative side of me that I need for writing. But why would I still feel this way, even after going through my own psychotherapy? Since this book isn't a memoir, I'll spare you the details. What's important is this: (1) I know my right brain is still a kid, and (2) *I'm writing in spite of these negative feelings.*

As I mentioned earlier, there are many reasons why we may feel reluctant to write. You may know of certain events in your life that have triggered creative blockage, or you may simply be aware of certain feelings or thoughts that well up whenever you think about starting a writing task.

Let's do another parallel monologue to get a quick read on some potential factors that may thwart your writing process. Respond first with your dominant hand, then with your nondominant hand.

<u>Dominant Hand</u>
Top Ten Reasons to Hurl Yourself into a Writer's Block

___ 1. Anger
___ 2. Anxiety
___ 3. Assertiveness problems
___ 4. Depression
___ 5. Fear of failure
___ 6. Fear of intimacy
___ 7. Fear of public exposure
___ 8. Fear of rejection
___ 9. Fear of success
__10. Perfectionism

<u>Nondominant Hand</u>
Top Ten Reasons to Hurl Yourself into a Writer's Block

___ 1. Anger
___ 2. Anxiety
___ 3. Assertiveness problems
___ 4. Depression
___ 5. Fear of failure

___ 6. Fear of intimacy
___ 7. Fear of public exposure
___ 8. Fear of rejection
___ 9. Fear of success
___10. Perfectionism

In response to this parallel monologue, my dominant hand checked off numbers 1 (anger) and 10 (perfectionism). I know that I can feel angry because I *think* I don't have enough time to write, and I know that perfectionism can paralyze me if I don't remember Anne Lamott's edict about simply writing an SFD ("shitty first draft"). Interestingly, my nondominant hand checked the items about anxiety (number 2) and depression (number 4). However, that side of my brain also checked off numbers 3 (assertiveness problems), 7 (fear of exposure), and 9 (fear of success). In other words, the right side of my brain still remembers my struggles with anxiety and depression, as well as how hard I had to work to move down the continuum of passivity to assertiveness in order to feel okay about saying "no" to others so I'd have time to write. My right brain, being the vessel of negative memories, also doesn't like the idea of being scrutinized—hence, the fear of exposure and success (even though my left brain is quite capable of handling all that).

Glance through your responses to this parallel monologue, and notice any trends or discrepancies between the two sides of the brain. Be aware that your responses—regardless of how outlandish they are—may be clues to unlocking the secrets of your writing process. For example, I once worked with a client who had over 4,000 references for her dissertation project, but still could not bring herself to begin writing. As she explored her obvious need to "have all the answers," it soon became apparent that the right side of her brain was still engaged in battle with a former English instructor who'd publicly humiliated her for "not having all the correct information," and this battle was in turn connected to the client's internal battle with her hypercritical mother, from whom the client could never glean approval. Although this is an extreme case of overresearching, it's not the only case I've come across.

Keep in mind that regardless of how extreme your procrastination has been in terms of your writing, you can still win the battle with writer's block—which, by the way, comes in three varieties.

Triptych of Angst: The Three Types of Writer's Block

Although most people think of writer's block as one concept, there are actually three types of writer's block. You may experience only one or two types, or if you're really lucky like me, you can have all three!

In private sessions and in workshops across the country, I have seen so many reasons why writers get blocked, so I have taken the liberty of categorizing them as follows: task related, biochemically related, and person related. Although we will examine each type of writer's block separately, be aware that there is a great deal of overlap among these three categories, so it is common to experience at least two of the three types. (I rarely see a client who has only one of these types of writer's block.)

Task-related writer's block is just that: a blockage that occurs primarily as a result of issues directly related to the writing project, such as difficulty in selecting, narrowing, or organizing a topic; tracking a novel's subplots; research problems; or difficulty accepting the need for revisions.

Let's respond to the following parallel monologue, and see if there are any relevant issues related to this type of writer's block. Respond first with your dominant hand, then with your nondominant hand.

<u>Dominant Hand</u>
Top Ten Task-Related Reasons Not to Start Writing

___ 1. It's too overwhelming.
___ 2. I don't have time.
___ 3. I need a big block of time.
___ 4. I don't have an organized writing area.
___ 5. I don't know how to organize the writing project.
___ 6. I can't pick a topic.
___ 7. I can't narrow the topic.
___ 8. I can't expand the topic.
___ 9. I need more training in the craft of writing.
___10. Other:_____

<u>Nondominant Hand</u>
Top Ten Task-Related Reasons Not to Start Writing

___ 1. It's too overwhelming.

___ 2. I don't have time.

___ 3. I need a big block of time.

___ 4. I don't have an organized writing area.

___ 5. I don't know how to organize the writing project.

___ 6. I can't pick a topic.

___ 7. I can't narrow the topic.

___ 8. I can't expand the topic.

___ 9. I need more training in the craft of writing.

___10. Other:_____

My responses to this exercise were quite divergent. With my dominant hand, I checked only number 1 (overwhelmed). Well, writing is an overwhelming process. You have to (1) shut out the entire world, (2) go internal, and (3) find something to say. Any one of those three steps can trip me up. I love to write, but it's intense work, and I have to give up other activities in order to spend time with the Muse.

My nondominant hand (which checked numbers 1, 2, 3, 4, and 5) agrees, but more due to feeling overwhelmed emotionally, rather than intellectually. Of course, my all-or-nothing right brain thinks I have "no time to write," that I need "a big block of time," that I don't have an "organized writing area," and that I don't know "how to organize writing projects." These are all reflections of my more childlike right brain, which demands that *writing should be fun, not hard work!*

Although I now have confidence that I can maintain an organized writing area, my right brain doesn't agree. Although my logical left brain knows that maintaining a visually appealing and comfortable writing area is under my control, my more childlike right brain still thinks that chaos will occur, no matter what I do. Yes, there is that problem with entropy: papers start to pile up—for me, it's inevitable—but my left brain knows how to organize them in a flash if I have to. And, at some point, when my right brain is riding a wave of panic, my left brain says, "Okay, now you're geting on your own nerves, so it's probably a good time to get organized."

In terms of organizing a writing project, my logical left brain knows that I taught English composition for seven years. If there's one thing I learned from grading fifty papers every week, it's that there is no one perfect way to organize a writing project. Au contraire—there are usually so many different ways to organize a task that we get overwhelmed just thinking about all the possibilities. An organizational strategy is just that—a strategy, a blueprint: If the dining room doesn't work there, just move it before you finish constructing the house. In other words, make a choice—any choice—and go for it. Allow yourself the right to be flexible. Once you begin to explore an organizational strategy for your writing project, you'll know what to do: ditch it, change it, or just do it.

For example, today I'm working on Chapter 6 of this book. I've completed Chapters 1, 3, 4, 5, and part of Chapter 10. I am definitely avoiding revising Chapter 2 because the material is complex and difficult to distill into a good read. Chapters 7, 8, and 9 are fully outlined and partially typed. This may not be the way other writers organize their projects, but sometimes I need to do things this way when I'm short on time and have to rely on whatever mood I'm in to eek out chunks of writing here and there. Sure, I'll need to go back and revise and make sure that things flow from chapter to chapter, but at least I'm working on my goal of completing this book.

This patchwork quilt method obviously does not work for everyone, or for every project. For example, when I am working with high school or college students stymied by their latest term papers, I'll offer a more structured format called "Managing the Writing Process" as a blueprint for at least starting the project. Most neophyte writers appreciate this outline, especially in terms of understanding that the two sides of the brain reign over different parts of the writing process. The corpus callosum, that gnarly cord between the right and left brain, tends to serve more as a barrier than a bridge. That's why it's so frustrating to stop and look up the spelling of a word or a reference (left brain work) while you're in the process of creating sentences to express your ideas (right brain work).

The answer is: Don't revise while you are writing (unless, of course, that comes easily to you). *Try to engage in only one step of the writing process at a time.* Keep five separate notebooks, one for each step of the writing process—but only use one notebook at a time. For example, if you think of a great sentence, go ahead and jot it down in notebook number 4. Maybe that's the only sentence you have today, so you switch over to notebook number 1 and start brainstorming by jotting down ideas or using a *spoke outline* (draw a circle or bicycle wheel with your topic in the center, and then make 4 or 5 "spokes"; not 100!—emanating from the bicycle wheel's hub, then jot down as quickly as possible on each spoke any ideas that come to you; the idea here is to brainstorm main ideas for your paper without getting caught up in details). When you switch from one notebook to another, you choose which side of your brain is most ready to write on that given day.

Managing the Writing Process:
Why Two Brains Are Better Than One

Brain Hemisphere	Procedure	Process
Right	Brainstorm/Spoke outline	Prewriting
Left	Select ideas/Order of ideas	Prewriting
Left	Read/Select sources and quotations	Prewriting
Right	Write sentences (don't stop to edit)	Writing
Left	Editing	Rewriting

Estimated Time	Procedure	Actual Time	Reward Time
_____	1._____	_____	_____
_____	2._____	_____	_____
_____	3._____	_____	_____
_____	4._____	_____	_____
_____	5._____	_____	_____

Current mood:
__anxious __highly focused __moderately focused __unfocused

Desired mood:
__anxious __highly focused __moderately focused __unfocused
To change mood: To energize_____ To relax_____

Since college students are well-known for pulling all-nighters and for not being aware of their mood states when they are trying to write, this chart can be especially helpful in strategizing a paper that has to be done ASAP. Due to the inherent anxiety associated with procrastination, the brain gets a bit rattled by 2 A.M., and students may find that they "can't think straight." What I usually advise is this: (1) Make a resolution to use the techniques in this book to avoid procrastination next time, and (2) make a spoke outline ASAP.

For example, here's a spoke outline for a paper on *How I Spent My Summer Vacation*.

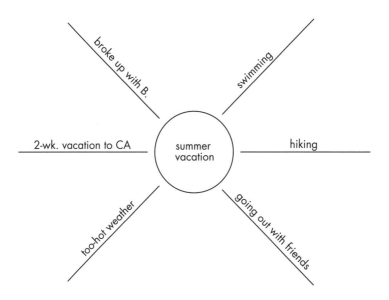

Here's another spoke outline, this time on *The Catcher in the Rye*.

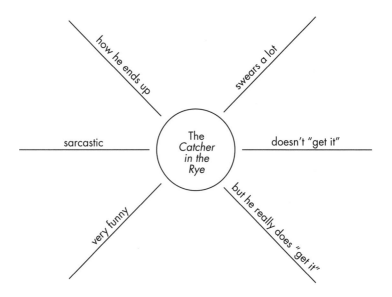

This model can also be helpful to writers of fiction (or nonfiction). For example, here's a spoke outline for getting started on a novel.

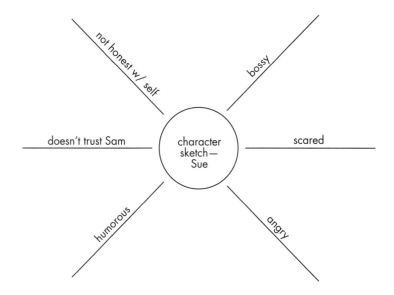

Once you've allowed yourself the luxury of just brainstorming like this—without branching off into distracting details—you may often find that your main ideas are right there on the spoke outline. You may decide to try to organize your writing project at that point (if you're in a left-brain mood), or you may decide to take an idea off one spoke of the outline and explore it. Either way, you've started the process of writing!

In addition, three books (written by current and former literary agents) are especially helpful in understanding the process of writing and revising: *Self-Editing for Fiction Writers* (by Renni Browne and Dave King), and *The First Five Pages* and *The Plot Thickens* (both by Noah Lukeman). These books are most helpful for task-related writer's block.

Now let's take a look at the second type of writer's block: *biochemically related writer's block*. Although this type frequently overlaps with task-related blockage, and while some of the task-related solutions we discussed may work, biochemically related writer's block is specifically tied to neurochemistry.

Let's explore this further. Try to answer the parallel monologue that follows, first with your dominant hand, then with your nondominant hand.

Dominant Hand
Top Ten Biochemically Related Reasons to Avoid Writing

___ 1. I can't concentrate enough to write.
___ 2. I don't have the energy to write.
___ 3. I'm too depressed to write.

___ 4. I'm too anxious to write.

___ 5. My first draft has to be perfect.

___ 6. I can't stop researching.

___ 7. I feel paralyzed and don't know where to start.

___ 8. I try to prewrite, write, and rewrite simultaneously.

___ 9. I can't stand the thought of revising.

___10. I can't get started unless I'm facing the wrong end of a deadline.

Nondominant Hand

Top Ten Biochemically Related Reasons to Avoid Writing

___ 1. I can't concentrate enough to write.

___ 2. I don't have the energy to write.

___ 3. I'm too depressed to write.

___ 4. I'm too anxious to write.

___ 5. My first draft has to be perfect.

___ 6. I can't stop researching.

___ 7. I feel paralyzed and don't know where to start.

___ 8. I try to prewrite, write, and rewrite simultaneously.

___ 9. I can't stand the thought of revising.

___10. I can't get started unless I'm facing the wrong end of a deadline.

My responses to this exercise held the usual discrepancies. With my dominant hand, I checked off numbers 1, 2, and 10. Of course, I often feel that I don't have the energy or concentration to write—hence, my need for that adrenaline rush inflicted by the threat of a deadline.

However, with my nondominant hand, I checked off not only numbers 1, 2, 3, 4, and 10 (my right brain just won't let go of those old battles with anxiety and depression!), but also numbers 6 (overresearching/perfectionism) and 7 (paralyzed/frozen creativity)—both of which reflect my right brain's all-or-nothing mentality.

Peruse your responses, and take note of any trends or surprising answers. Keep in mind that this is not a clinical diagnostic checklist, but merely an exercise to get you thinking about what blocks you. No matter which items you checked, *it does not automatically mean that you have a biochemical deficit or imbalance* (although it may be worth exploring with a licensed psychotherapist and/or psychopharmacologist if the behavioral techniques in this book aren't ultimately helpful).

For example, I have worked with many clients who have struggled with issues such as depression, anxiety, seasonal affective disorder (SAD), attention-deficit/hyperactivity disorder (AD/HD), obsessive-compulsive disorder (OCD), and/or post-traumatic stress disorder (PTSD). Each of these disorders involves an imbalance in one or more brain chemicals (such as serotonin, dopamine, and norepinephrine) that are necessary for focus, concentration, and motivation.

These clients may also have task-related writer's block, which often overlaps with biochemically related writer's block. For example, in response to the potentially "biochemical" factors listed here, many of my clients with AD/HD might check numbers

1 (trouble concentrating), 6 (overresearching), 8 (organizing, writing, and editing simultaneously), and 10 (needing a deadline to get motivated). Usually, writers with AD/HD can't focus unless they are in a distraction-free environment. Additionally, they often can't get motivated without the adrenaline rush incited by a deadline (they don't call it a *dead*line for nothing). For all intents and purposes, that adrenaline rush of panic might as well be a prescription for Ritalin or Adderall (both stimulant medications that may help with AD/HD).

Additionally, people with AD/HD tend to overresearch, especially if they're working online, because they get interested— aka, distracted—by so many different aspects of a topic. Instead of gathering just the facts needed to write, they may zip from one Web site to the next, with each Web site offering fascinating facts and further Web links that stray farther and farther from the writing topic. In this situation, it helps to set a timer for twenty-minute intervals, to remind the writer to stay on task. Interesting, but unrelated, Web sites can be jotted down for further exploration at a later date. (Exploring these Web sites that are just for fun may also serve as "reward" time for remaining on task for the assigned writing project.)

Writers with AD/HD also tend to prewrite, write, and rewrite simultaneously, because they tend to see the whole writing project in their heads all at the same time, so it's hard to separate ideas into simple, linear steps that others can follow. Additionally, because people with AD/HD tend to be more creative, they are often flooded with fascinating, sometimes interrelated ideas. One solution for this flood of ideas is to keep two notebooks handy:

one for ideas about your writing topic, and one for interesting but unrelated ideas to explore later.

If these issues sound familiar to you, *it does not necessarily mean that you have AD/HD.* Many writers are more right-brained, so they tend to think in terms of the whole, not the parts, of a story. Additionally, many writers struggle with these issues because they have a thinking style that is more divergent (think of everything all at once, including digressions) than convergent (think of ideas in hierarchical order, so they converge to your main point). In other words, writers are creative, so of course they digress! (The only way to know if you have AD/HD is to seek an assessment from a qualified, licensed mental health professional.)

Similarly, my clients with OCD might check off numbers 4 (anxiety), 5 (perfectionism), and 6 (overresearching). This is because people with OCD, ruled by the Medusa of perfectionism, often feel anxious about not getting all the facts—and I do mean all of them.

In contrast, when I'm working with writers who have PTSD, they might check numbers 1 (concentration problems), 4 (anxiety), and 7 (feeling paralyzed). People who have suffered a trauma (or chronic neglect) often cannot concentrate because they may be hypervigilant—their sympathetic nervous systems are overly activated, always on guard in case of "attack." Clients with PTSD usually have anxiety over their past—and fear of future—negative experiences, and they may feel paralyzed with writer's block because, like the deer in the headlights, they may freeze up because they still haven't learned how to behave proactively (versus reactively) in anxiety-provoking situations. What they tend to need more than anything to overcome writer's block is a feeling of *safety*, however that may be defined.

If you suspect that you have—or have already been diagnosed with—AD/HD, OCD, PTSD, or any other disorder that involves biochemical as well as psychological factors, it would be wise to seek counseling from a competent psychotherapist and/or medical intervention from a competent psychopharmacologist (the American Psychological Association and the American Psychiatric Association both maintain Web sites listing their ethical members who are in good standing). Additionally, some psychotherapists are trained in eye movement desensitization and reprocessing (EMDR), which is a relatively new therapeutic approach (developed in 1989) involving bilateral stimulation of both the right and left sides of the brain. (As you can see on the EMDR Web site, since EMDR is such an intensive approach, results can be achieved more quickly, but individuals must be screened by an EMDR-trained clinician prior to treatment. Although the research results on the use of EMDR have been generally quite positive, it is still considered by many professionals to be an "experimental" approach to therapy for issues such as trauma, depression, anxiety, and "performance enhancement" for creative individuals.)

On the other hand, all of these issues on the biochemically related reasons to avoid writing checklist can also be triggered by other issues, such as learning disabilities or psychological factors that have nothing to do with AD/HD, OCD, PTSD, or any other biochemically related syndromes. In the next section, we will review person-related writer's block, which often accounts for a large percentage of problems with creative blockage—either in combination with biochemically related or task-related writer's block.

Person-related writer's block involves feelings about other people (interpersonal factors) or feelings within and about ourselves (intrapersonal factors). Again, these factors may overlap with task-related or biochemically related issues, but let's take a look inside and respond to this next parallel monologue. Start with your dominant hand, and then switch to your nondominant hand.

Dominant Hand
Top Ten Person-Related Reasons Not to Start Writing

___ 1. I get nervous just thinking about writing.

___ 2. I'm reluctant to write because it won't be good enough.

___ 3. Who would want to read what I have to say?

___ 4. What if my book is successful?

___ 5. If I started writing,_____would resent it.

___ 6. If I started writing, I'd have to give up_____.

___ 7. If I started writing, I'd have to start_____.

___ 8. If I started writing, it would affect my relationship with_____.

___ 9. If I started writing, it would affect my job/household duties by_____.

___10. If I started writing, then *they* (   ) might think_____.

<u>Nondominant Hand</u>

Top Ten Person-Related Reasons Not to Start Writing

___ 1. I get nervous just thinking about writing.

___ 2. I'm reluctant to write because it won't be good enough.

___ 3. Who would want to read what I have to say?

___ 4. What if my book is successful?

___ 5. If I started writing,_____would resent it.

___ 6. If I started writing, I'd have to give up_____.

___ 7. If I started writing, I'd have to start_____.

___ 8. If I started writing, it would affect my relationship with_____.

___ 9. If I started writing, it would affect my job/household duties by_____.

___10. If I started writing, then *they* (   ) might think_____.

As usual, my responses were quite different when I switched hands. First, my dominant hand checked off number 6 (I'd have to give up "being so organized in other areas of my life"). These responses reflect my reluctance to let go of some of the control issues I have about keeping up with all of my other responsibilities outside of writing.

The other side of my brain has its own litany of excuses. My nondominant hand checked off numbers 1 (nervousness), 4 (fear of success), 5 ("my loved ones" would resent my writing), 6 (I'd have to give up "being comfortable"), 7 (I'd have to start "stopping being so nervous"), and 8 (writing would affect my relationship with myself—"I could get scared"). Whew—any one of these would be enough to block even the most undaunted writer. The fact is, my loved ones are very supportive of my writing, so chances are my right brain is thinking of my childhood list, rather than my current list, of so-called loved ones.

All the items I checked about being nervous, uncomfortable, and scared are familiar to me as typical of my right brain's approach to the writing process. However, in spite of all that, I have been able to reassure my right brain that those negative emotions are simply the fading reverberations of old childhood feelings—and that time in my life is over. In my adult life now, I am safe, I have surrounded myself with my own family and loving friends, and I am in control of my destiny.

As you examine your responses to these two lists, you'll probably sense that the items are related to various saboteurs of the creative spirit: anxiety (numbers 1, 8, and 10), fear of failure or rejection (numbers 2, 3, 9, and 10), perfectionism (numbers 2 and 10), fear of success (numbers 4 and 10), codependence and lack of assertiveness with others (numbers 5 and 8), fear of change and letting go of control (numbers 6, 7, and 9), and our all-time favorites, guilt ("I did something wrong") and shame ("I am bad because I did something wrong"), as exemplified by numbers 2, 3, and 10.

These issues may emanate from a variety of interpersonal or intrapersonal sources. For example, I have worked with many writers who were still reeling from feelings of rejection after being sharply criticized and/or humiliated by parents, siblings, teachers, academic advisors, editors, and just about anybody else who can get their hands on our psyches. Sometimes, these shaming events from the past are related to writing, and sometimes not.

When I'm working with a client who is procrastinating or blocked regarding academic work, I often discover that the teacher or dissertation advisor has unwittingly triggered a re-enactment of old childhood dynamics for the client. For example, the editor or professor may share certain personality traits with the client's father, mother, or ex-spouse. What happens, of course, is that the client begins to feel too resentful, powerless, angry, or vulnerable to approach the writing process. Some writers still carry from childhood an old message that it's not acceptable to fail, or to outshine your parents, or to make too much money if you're successful.

These and many other feelings that you may carry within yourself can trigger an intrapersonal writer's block in the sense that you may still be fighting—internally—the old battles with *them*. As Mildred Newman and Bernard Berkowitz so aptly state in one of the first good self-help books, *How to Take Charge of Your Life*:

> *Would you believe*
> That when you stab yourself
> "They" bleed?
>
> Would you believe
> That when you fall on your face
> "They" 'll be sorry?

The trick is to realize that there was a reason we couldn't win those old battles. Usually, the other people weren't playing by the same set of rules, and they didn't play fair. Now, in our adult lives, we can step back and begin to see that we no longer need to project these old issues onto perceived authority figures, because those old battles aren't worth fighting anymore. (See Eliana Gil's *Outgrowing the Pain* for a good discussion of this dynamic.)

We now have a choice that perhaps we didn't have *back then.* Now, we can be assertive and demand to be respected, or we can walk away and find a new situation that suits us better in terms of completing a writing project. (Dr. Amy Stark explores these issues in terms of job-related writing projects in her book *Because I Said So: Recognize the Influence of Childhood Dynamics on Office Politics and Take Charge of Your Career.*)

If, however, you still find yourself blocked, it may be advisable to consult with a licensed psychotherapist to help you let go of these old feelings. This is true especially if you are blocked about writing something that is fully or semiautobiographical. Aside from the need to avoid "the autobiographical trap" (i.e., writing it exactly as it happened, even if it doesn't create an effective plot line or even if it doesn't hold universal appeal), you may also be uncomfortable with the material, even though you truly want to write about it. One option is to write about the events in third person, past tense—as if it happened to someone else, not you. This would give you the most emotional distance from the subject matter you may be avoiding. You may choose to leave your story, novel, essay, or poem in third person, or, when you're ready, you may move from second person or even into first person, perhaps even into present tense. These options will give you less emotional distance, of course, but more immediacy and intensity in the writing. (For some exercises on this, consult the section on *psychoautobiographical writing* in Chapter 6 of *The Tomorrow Trap: Unlocking the Secrets of the Procrastination-Protection Syndrome,* by yours truly.)

However, if you are writing about highly charged events that had a negative impact on you, it may be advisable to consult with a licensed psychotherapist prior to engaging in any autobiographical writing so that you can approach the material safely and comfortably. For example, in *Fire in the Soul*, Dr. Joan Borysenko writes about a Holocaust survivor who could only speak in third person about the horrors he'd witnessed—until he had worked through the trauma, at which point he could discuss his experiences in first person.

On the other hand, writing about troubling experiences, if done in a safe and appropriate manner, may have therapeutic value. Dr. James Pennebaker (*Opening Up* and *Writing to Heal*) has conducted extensive research to demonstrate the healing power of writing about stressful experiences, and the American Psychological Association has published a book on the therapeutic power of writing (*The Writing Cure*, edited by Stephen Lepore and Joshua Smyth). However, when dealing with autobiographical material, the most important factor to consider is your level of comfort—you can always wait to write that book at a later date, once you've gained perspective and some emotional distance from the material.

One last tip on writing autobiographical material: If you're concerned about being sued for libel (writing false material about an actual person) or for invasion of privacy (writing any material, true or false, about a private individual in such a way that it causes damage to that person or that person's career), it is best to consult with an intellectual property rights attorney to see how much you may need to conceal identities and change identifying information in order to protect yourself from potential legal action if you choose to publish your work.

Setting Sail for the Seven Seas of Creativity

Whether your writing is autobiographical or not, when it comes to starting your writing project, you may choose any of the bi-vocal techniques presented thus far in this book. Pick the charts and methods that are most appealing to you right now. Task-sprinting, selecting a comfortable place and time to write, and giving yourself permission to write an SFD would all be great places to start. You may use the charts in previous chapters, or perhaps skip ahead to Chapter 10 if you want to jump-start your Ten-Day Writing Plan now.

On the other hand, if you've already started writing, but are stuck somewhere in the middle of your project and can't seem to get back to it, then the next chapter is for you. Although nonwriters usually don't understand why we have trouble picking up pen and paper on a project that may already be well under way, there are reasons why we stop midstream. In Chapter 7, we'll explore these reasons and find some ways to get that stream of creativity flowing once again—the waters may be choppy at first, but we'll learn new ways to navigate the writing process so we can be in charge of our destinies as writers.

Ready to set sail?

continuing to write:
the plot as "bribe"

The plot is just a bribe to keep them reading.

—Kurt Vonnegut, *Case Western Reserve University, 1985*

It's like making a movie: All sorts of accidental things will happen after you've set up the cameras. So you get lucky. Something will happen at the edge of the set and perhaps you start to go with that; you get some footage of that. You come into it accidentally. You set the story in motion, and as you're watching this thing begin, all these opportunities will show up.

—Kurt Vonnegut, *Writers on Writing*

Getting Back on Track

So you're in pursuit of it all—life, liberty, happiness, education, a good relationship, and somewhere in there, a writing career.

You're also in the middle of a writing project. You finally got it started, but now you want to keep moving toward the finish line. Sometimes it's hard to continue writing because:

You already know it all in your head, and you just don't feel like writing it down.
Or . . .
You have no idea where to go next in this writing project.
Or . . .
Both.

Either way, it's a toss up as to how you'll get back into the writing process. Maybe you dropped the ball a few days ago, or a month ago, or a year ago. So how do you get back on track?

There are numerous factors that keep us from returning to our writing projects—whether they are cherished novels or required papers. I have worked with a number of writers who had abandoned cherished writing projects—or dissertations—for more than a decade. In every case, the writers would have some ambivalence about reimmersing themselves in their abandoned projects. Sometimes, these writers were conflicted about the actual task, and sometimes their blockage was tethered to intrapersonal or interpersonal issues.

Let's try a parallel monologue to see what each of our voices has to say about all this.

Dominant Hand

When I think of continuing to work on a writing task, I feel:_____.

Nondominant Hand

When I think of continuing to work on a writing task, I feel:_____.

I did this exercise on two different occasions over the course of a month or so, and my responses, though different, were amazingly consistent over time. With my dominant hand, I first wrote "tired," and on the second occasion I wrote "exhausted." Both of these responses reflect that I was slightly overcommitted during this past month, so of course the prospect of writing felt tiring in advance. However, with my nondominant hand, on the first occasion, I wrote that I felt "mad—it takes too long! I want to have more fun now," and on the second occasion I wrote that I felt "mad—I just want to play." Again, these responses are consistent, and both reflect the fact that I was working too much during that busy month.

Glance at your responses to this parallel monologue, and take note of any trends or discrepancies. Then, respond to this next, more detailed, parallel monologue so we can discern which factors may be thwarting your attempts to return to your writing project.

Dominant Hand
Top Ten Reasons I Can't Get Back into Writing

___ 1. I feel like I've lost momentum.

___ 2. It's hard to immerse myself again—I need a big block of time.

___ 3. I feel like I don't know where to go next.

___ 4. I don't want to do any more research.

___ 5. I need to do more research.

___ 6. My loved ones are complaining that I spend too much time writing.

___ 7. My job/schedule/priorities have changed.

___ 8. I've lost interest.

___ 9. I feel discouraged by someone's critique of my writing.

___10. The closer I get to the halfway point, the more panicky I feel about:_____.

Nondominant Hand
Top Ten Reasons I Can't Get Back into Writing

___ 1. I feel like I've lost momentum.

___ 2. It's hard to immerse myself again—I need a big block of time.

___ 3. I feel like I don't know where to go next.

___ 4. I don't want to do any more research.

___ 5. I need to do more research.

___ 6. My loved ones are complaining that I spend too much time writing.

___ 7. My job/schedule/priorities have changed.

_____ 8. I've lost interest.

_____ 9. I feel discouraged by someone's critique of my writing.

_____10. The closer I get to the halfway point, the more panicky
   I feel about:_____.

Again, my responses to this exercise were divergent. With my dominant hand, I checked off numbers 3 (don't know where to go next), 7 (changed priorities), and 10 (panicky about "not getting this book done!"). These answers all reflect the fact that, like any human being, I can get confused and lose my inner guidance if I'm not careful to challenge my notions about perfectionism (just start anywhere, even if it's just revising what I've already done), allow myself to use small chunks of time to write (no matter what my other new priorities are), and give myself permission to acknowledge that these small chunks of time will add up to a completed manuscript (all I have to do is put in the time, and it will get done).

In contrast, with my nondominant hand, I checked off numbers 1 (lost momentum), 2 (difficult to reimmerse myself, need big block of time), 5 (need to do more research), and 10 (panicky about "not getting enough fun!"). These responses reflect my perfectionistic, all-or-nothing right brain's belief that I need *intense momentum* (read: mania) to get started, that I have to find *just the right place* in the writing project to reimmerse myself, that I need *huge blocks of time and enormous piles of research* in front of me before I can assert my own ideas—and of course the fact that I will *never* have leisure time again once I start writing.

When I'm overwhelmed by these old feelings, I know that I need to engage in some interior dialogue. Most of the time, what my right brain wants is "fun," translated as "reward time" by my left brain—reward time that I'll get after I've spent even a small chunk of time writing.

Here, once again, is your opportunity to do the same. After glancing through your responses to the previous parallel monologue, focus on your current resistance about returning to your writing project. Then, try to respond to the following interior dialogue, and see if you can somehow give yourself whatever it is that you need in order to continue the writing process.

Interior Dialogue

Dominant hand: What do you need right now?

Nondominant hand:_____

Dominant hand: What would you need to be able to do this writing task?

Nondominant hand:_____

Dominant hand: Let me see if I can find a way to get you what you need. Maybe we can_____, or we could_____either now, or after twenty minutes of writing. Would that help?

Nondominant hand:_____

Dominant hand: Okay, then, are you ready to try this for a few minutes?

Nondominant hand:_____

Once again, if you need more of a jump-start, see how you respond to any of the following questions. Just answer the ones that resonate with you. Remember to use your nondominant hand to answer the questions posed by your dominant hand.

Extended Interior Dialogue

Potential questions for the dominant hand to pose to the nondominant hand:

Dominant Hand   Nondominant Hand

1. What's wrong?   _____

2. How are you feeling?   _____

3. What else are you feeling?   _____

4. What do you think about that?   _____

5. What do you need right now?   _____

6. What do you want right now?   _____

7. What else do you want right   _____
now?

8. What do you need to be able   _____
to complete this subtask?

9. What would it mean if you did   _____
this subtask?

10. Tell me more about that.   _____

11. What will you need after you   _____
complete the subtask?

12. What would you like to have   _____
after you complete the subtask?

13. What would you like to do   _____
after you complete the subtask?

14. What do you need to have as   _____
a reward for doing this?

15. What would you like to have as a reward for doing this? _____

16. Which part of the writing process do you feel like doing right now? _____

17. Which writing project do you feel like working on right now? _____

18. Which kind of mood are you in right now—and how can we change it? _____

19. How many minutes would you like to try writing today? _____

20. How many minutes of reward time do you need if you write today? _____

Now that your newly enlightened left brain has given your right brain what it needs—guidance and choices—you may find it's much easier to approach a twenty-minute block of writing time, or to use any of the techniques presented in Chapters 1 through 6. The point is to give yourself whatever you need to continue working on your writing project.

In the next chapter, we'll discuss some strategies for actually *completing* your writing project—because, yes, Virginia, there *is* a final clause.

CHAPTER 8

finishing writing projects:

always busy, never done

I have rewritten—often several times—

every word I have ever published.

My pencils outlast their erasers.

—Vladimir Nabokov

You are in the midst of a moving process. Nothing fails then. All goes on. Work is done. If good, you learn from it. If bad, you learn even more.

—Ray Bradbury

The Infinitely Receding Finish Line

Even though a project may be near completion, relatively easy to complete, or actually finished, you may still be unable to jettison that manuscript off of your desk and onto someone else's. In this chapter, you'll see that being unable to complete a writing project may be related to one or more of the following:

- The writer
- The writing task
- Known audience members
- Unknown audience members
- Agents
- Publishers
- Editors

I have worked with numerous writers who have stopped short of completing term papers, theses, dissertations, novels—you name it. In some cases, these unfinished writing projects meant that the clients could not graduate from college or graduate school. I have also worked with students and writers who have completed their writing tasks, but were unwilling to turn them in, usually because the writing wasn't "perfect." In these cases as well, the clients were often unable to obtain their diplomas.

However, with the appropriate interventions, these clients were able to choose their next course of action. Most of them chose to finish their projects. Among the few who chose not to finish their projects, most decided to change careers or take a new job instead—because, on some level, they really didn't want to have a law or medical degree or a B.A. in business or biology. (Quite often, they were simply fulfilling the dreams of one or both parents, rather than following their true career choices.) Either way, when it comes to the completion of your writing projects, you can decide to reach the finish line even though your right brain may be blocked by any number of issues.

Taking Steps Toward the Finish Line

By now, you probably know which issues are holding you back from completing your writing project. Let's take a closer look to see how you feel by using the following parallel monologue.

Dominant Hand
When I think of finishing a writing task, I feel_____.

Nondominant Hand
When I think of finishing a writing task, I feel_____.

My answers to this exercise indicate some ambivalence. With my dominant hand, I wrote "Okay, but stressed." This response reflects my left brain's realistic awareness that even large book projects can be completed, but the process can be stressful.

However, with my nondominant hand, I wrote "I don't know if it's good or not." What I meant by this was whether it's a good idea to complete the project—or not. When it comes to finishing a writing task and presenting it to the public, my more childlike right brain is usually asking, *"What if it's not good enough?"*

The point is, however, that I did finish the project: You're holding a copy of it right now.

As you review your responses to this exercise, keep in mind that you may get other responses at a later date, or regarding different projects. I have worked with many writers who were able to contain their fear of failure until it came down to the finish line. Some clients were concerned more about what certain people would think of their work, while others had more general concerns about readers' reactions or critics' reviews.

Let's see from whence your finish-line angst may spring. Try to respond to this next parallel monologue, first with your dominant hand, then with your nondominant hand.

Dominant Hand
Top Ten Reasons to Veer Away from the Finish Line

___ 1. I just don't feel like finishing this writing project.

___ 2. I'm worried about who will read this.

___ 3. I'll never get an agent anyway.

___ 4. I'll never get a publisher anyway.

___ 5. I fear the red pen of an editor.

___ 6. I don't want to let go of these characters—they're like part of my life.

___ 7. I don't know what I'll do once this project is no longer part of my life.

___ 8. I don't know when to stop researching.

___ 9. I don't know when to stop revising.

___10. If I finish, I don't know how I'll deal with
the consequences.

<u>Nondominant Hand</u>

Top Ten Reasons to Veer Away from the Finish Line

___ 1. I just don't feel like finishing this writing project.

___ 2. I'm worried about who will read this.

___ 3. I'll never get an agent anyway.

___ 4. I'll never get a publisher anyway.

___ 5. I fear the red pen of an editor.

___ 6. I don't want to let go of these characters—they're like
part of my life.

___ 7. I don't know what I'll do once this project is no longer
part of my life.

___ 8. I don't know when to stop researching.

___ 9. I don't know when to stop revising.

___10. If I finish, I don't know how I'll deal with
the consequences.

Once again, my responses weren't exactly consistent. With
my dominant hand, I checked off numbers 1 (don't feel like it), 5
(fear of editor's comments), and 9 (not sure when to stop revising).
These answers don't surprise me. As I try to write the last part of a
writing project, of course "I don't feel like it," because in my head I'm
already done with this task and ready to start a new one! In contrast,
my other two responses are more concerned with my fear that if I

don't write well enough by revising unto perfection, an unknown copyeditor won't understand what I'm trying to say, and he or she will distort my message. Ridiculous? Of course—especially since I have experience in working with editors and copyeditors.

Meanwhile, my nondominant hand had other complaints: numbers 1 (don't feel like it), 2 (worried about readership), 3 (never get an agent), 4 (never get a publisher), 5 (fear of editor's criticism), and 10 (concern about consequences of finishing). These responses reflect my childlike, all-or-nothing, irrational right brain's MO Naturally "I don't feel like it," because writing is hard work. Numbers 2 and 10 are related, as they both reflect my oh-so-human penchant for self-sabotage (e.g., *What if people don't like my book?*)

However, my responses to numbers 3, 4, and 5 are absurd: I already have a wonderful agent, a reputable publisher, and a very patient editor. On the other hand, I have to remind myself that the right side of the brain is dominant for emotion—which, as we all know, does not have to answer to the gods of logic.

As you take note of your responses to this exercise, be aware of any trends or surprising answers. For example, if you checked number 6, it may surprise you to realize that you don't want to finish your short story or novel because you don't want to let go of the characters yet. On the other hand, who says these characters can't turn up in another short story or novel? (For example, Elizabeth Berg wrote her novel *True to Form* after one of her readers said she wanted to know what happened to the main character from the previous novels!)

Another item that tends to surprise my clients is number 7: A writing project may feel so much a part of your life that you can't part with it. I once worked with a client who had been "finishing" a dissertation project—ever-present on his kitchen table—for nearly twenty-five years. The client had obtained numerous extensions on his deadline, of course, but whenever he thought about the kitchen table suddenly being empty, he'd feel an unnerving sense of loneliness.

The manuscript had been his unswerving companion for over two decades—starting right after his divorce. On some level, he knew that the manuscript wouldn't stand him up on a Saturday night or betray him in any way. On the other hand, it had kept him from dating and socializing for years, because he always "had to work on the dissertation." In a sense, the manuscript had been protecting him from further disappointment in the world of relationships. However, as the client began to realize that his writer's block was imprisoning him, not simply protecting him, he was able to begin working steadily on finishing his dissertation, and even began, slowly, to socialize again.

As you consider your thoughts and feelings about finishing your writing projects, keep in mind that you can try any of the techniques presented in previous chapters. Whether it's starting with a twenty-minute commitment on your lunch hour, or sitting down with a friend to review what you've already written, you can complete the task whenever you're ready. One step at a time.

In the next chapter, we'll examine what happens after you've taken that final step. We'll turn our focus away from writing and toward the process of publication. And it's on to the slush pile from there. . . .

CHAPTER 9

publishing writing projects:

from panic to press release

It's much more important to write than to be written about.

—Gabriel Garcia Marquez

Whenever I feel uneasy about my writing, I think:
What would be the response of the people
in the book if they read the book?
That's my way of staying on track.
Those are the people for whom I write.

—Toni Morrison

Writing: It's All about You

As these two quotations from Marquez and Morrison illustrate, we need to write for ourselves first and foremost. To truly put yourself on the page—and what else is writing but that—you must keep your audience and the critics at bay. Whether you're writing fiction or nonfiction, you might think of your readers perhaps during the revision process, depending on the market for your book. But when you first put pen to page, it's important to feel unfettered by the opinions of others. What you have to say is yours, and only you can express it in a way that your intuition tells you is best.

So let's say you did just that. You've finished your manuscript and revised it to the point where it is ready to face the world of publication. Whether it's a poem sent to a literary magazine, a first novel sent to a prestigious literary publisher, or a nonfiction book sent to a publisher of serious nonfiction, you are now thrust into another world. Now comes the process of writing query letters and novel synopses, compiling book proposals, seeking out agents or publishers, and working effectively with editors. In this chapter, you'll learn how to adjust your expectations about the world of publishing, which will make it more likely that the next time you go to your favorite bookstore, it will be for your *own* book signing!

Publishing: It's All about Them?

As we move from being writers to being published authors, the most important shift involves perspective: Suddenly, the camera is facing us from another direction.

Let's take a look at the way you feel about publishing your work, and then focus on some strategies to help you put your best book forward. Respond as quickly as possible to the following parallel monologue, first with your dominant hand and then with your nondominant hand.

Dominant Hand
When I think of publishing my work, I feel_____.

Nondominant Hand
When I think of publishing my work, I feel_____.

My answers to this exercise were as follows: With my dominant hand, I wrote "pretty good," and with my nondominant hand, I wrote, "nervous, but okay." These responses reflect the fact that I have published my work before—and lived to tell about it. My right brain, of course, is hesitant as always, but you can tell which side of my brain won the battle on this one!

Notice your responses, and try to detect any trends or divergent reactions. There are many reasons why writers may shun publication, even though they may crave it. Let's respond to the top ten lists below, and see if we can discern just exactly what is holding us back from that first book signing.

<u>Dominant Hand</u>

Top Ten Reasons to Avoid Publication

___ 1. It's overwhelming to think about writing a book proposal.

___ 2. It's overwhelming to think about writing a novel synopsis.

___ 3. It's overwhelming to think about writing a query letter.

___ 4. It's overwhelming to think about writing to an agent.

___ 5. It's overwhelming to think about writing to an editor.

___ 6. It's overwhelming to think about writing to a publisher.

___ 7. I don't know how to select an agent.

___ 8. I don't know how to select a publisher.

___ 9. I don't know which editor to target at a given publishing house.

___10. I don't know how my book will be marketed.

<u>Nondominant Hand</u>

Top Ten Reasons to Avoid Publication

___ 1. It's overwhelming to think about writing a book proposal.

___ 2. It's overwhelming to think about writing a novel synopsis.

___ 3. It's overwhelming to think about writing a query letter.

___ 4. It's overwhelming to think about writing to an agent.

___ 5. It's overwhelming to think about writing to an editor.

___ 6. It's overwhelming to think about writing to a publisher.

___ 7. I don't know how to select an agent.

___ 8. I don't know how to select a publisher.

___ 9. I don't know which editor to target at a given publishing house.

___10. I don't know how my book will be marketed.

In my responses to this exercise, I surprised myself. With my dominant hand, I checked off numbers 1 and 2 (book proposals and novel synopses are overwhelming), as well as number 10 (uncertainty about how my book will be marketed). Although I already know how to write book proposals, as well as novel synopses, I have to admit that I still get edgy when I have to compose either one—like most writers, I have trouble deciding what to leave in and what to leave out.

The fact that I checked number 10 is reminiscent of my control issues. I want everyone to buy my books, so I don't want to limit the ways in which they are marketed, but I also can't decide on the best ways to market them. Never mind that publishers have marketing experts who have done this successfully, hundreds of times—the thought of giving over control to them is difficult for me, even though it's a necessity. I know they'll ask for my input, too, and I'll give it to them, but I'm never really sure if I've left out a major chunk of information that could have boosted the sales of my book (read: perfectionism strikes again!).

As if that weren't enough to stress out about, with my nondominant hand, I checked off numbers 1 through 10. Yes, *all of them*—as would befit my all-or-nothing right brain, I suppose. It's overwhelming to write proposals, synopses, and query letters because my right brain thinks that I might say *the wrong thing*, and then my book will *never* get published. It's also overwhelming to write to important, powerful "authority figures" like agents and editors and publishers (*lions, and tigers, and bears, oh my*). My right brain still feels intimidated, even though I have worked well with these professionals in the past.

It's also surprising that my less-than-confident right brain checked off the items related to not knowing how to target the right agents, publishers, and editors, since I now know exactly how to do this. Finally, it comes as no surprise that my right brain also has control issues about how and where my book will be marketed— because, hey, you just never know what'll happen next, and the thought of having a vote in the process of marketing doesn't even occur to that childlike, less-than-empowered right side of my brain.

As you review your responses to this parallel monologue, try to remember that as writers, we tend to have similar thoughts as we approach the publishing process. We've already written what we have to say, and now we have to convince someone else that what we wrote is publishable material. Rule number one: *Agents, editors, and publishers are human beings, with their own flaws and personal preferences. What one agent will reject, another will scoop up like a jewel among ashes.*

Or, perhaps I should say, like a jewel among the rubble. You probably already know this, but if you don't, here's the truth. Do you know what agents and editors call the daily onslaught of unsolicited manuscripts delivered at their doors? They call it "the slush pile." I was appalled when I first heard this, until I realized how many manuscripts editors and agents receive on any given day. Of course, I thought, "How can they call my work part of a *slush pile*?"

However, after I got over my initial reaction to the term, I realized that, like everyone else who is overwhelmed on the job, agents and editors have to use some kind of gallows humor to get by, so I resolved to forgive them. Instead of pouting, I decided to find out the best way to keep my manuscripts from ending up in that so-called slush pile. I decided to find out how to get my work directly into the hands of someone who could make it happen!

The best way to make sure your manuscript ends up in the right hands is to target agents, editors, and publishers who are most likely to be interested in your work. This means going beyond *Literary Marketplace*, which is simply an annual list of literary agents and publishers. It means looking at books that are similar in topic, tone, and/or genre, checking the acknowledgments pages for the authors' expression of appreciation to their agents and editors, and targeting these professionals first. It means buying the annual edition of Jeff Herman's *Guide to Book Publishers, Editors, and Literary Agents,* which includes interviews with hundreds of agents, editors, and publishers so you can get a feel for their preferences. Herman's book also contains a number of excellent chapters on how to write query letters, how to ease into the world of publishing, and how to write book proposals, whether it's before or after you've written the book. (In general, agents and editors usually prefer that you submit a nonfiction book proposal before you've written the book. However, with fiction, editors and agents usually won't look at a novel until it's completed, and then they'll want a novel synopsis as well.)

Right now, you're probably overwhelmed just hearing all this. If so, you might try the *Author 101* series published by Adams Media. The series includes four books on the process of writing and getting published—all in a reader-friendly format.

As writers, we are naturally going to feel indignant: *"Hey, I worked really hard on this manuscript, and now I have to do more work?"* Additionally, most of us aren't adept at promoting ourselves or our writing—we're writers, not publicists, marketing executives, or sales professionals! How can they expect us to do all this?

Well, the answer is, they do—because they can. Publishing, remember, is about making a profit. It's a business. Most writers have trouble making this transition, but it is possible to do so without sacrificing your identity as a creative person with integrity.

Numerous guides are available to give further information that goes beyond the scope of this book. Again, you may find the *Author 101* series helpful. You may also want to review Elizabeth Lyon's book *Nonfiction Book Proposals Anybody Can Write* to get an overview of the process of writing query letters, query packages (which may include a sample chapter and book outline), and book proposals. Similarly, Noah Lukeman's two books, *The Plot Thickens* and *The First Five Pages: A Writer's Guide to Staying Out of the Rejection Pile*, are excellent resources for preparing manuscripts for successful publication.

Yes, the publication industry can be difficult to navigate. But with the right ship and the right sails, you can do this. The important thing to remember is that agents, editors, and publishers have different tastes in books. For example, when I was seeking a publisher for my first book (*The Tomorrow Trap: Unlocking the Secrets of the Procrastination-Protection Syndrome*), I received many letters from agents and editors declining to review the proposal. Most of them were form letters, giving reasons such as, "we just published a book on this topic" or "not quite right for our spring (or fall) list."

Then, one day, I was fortunate enough to receive not just one, but *two* letters of rejection in the mail. The first one said something unusually and unnecessarily scathing, like "this wouldn't even make a good magazine article" (gee, do you think I touched a nerve or something?). The second one said something to the effect of "What a great idea for a book, but I'm sorry we don't to self-help anymore—try so-and-so over at St. Martin's Press, and best of luck to you!" Finally, the editor who actually accepted my book called me as soon as she received my query letter and said, "I love your book. What do I have to do to buy it?" Go figure.

What this means is: Keep throwing it out there until it sticks to somebody's wall, because eventually you'll hit the right target. Consider the roots of the word *reject*: *jacere*, the Latin word meaning "to throw," and *rejicere*, meaning "to throw or fling back." Thus, to reject is to throw something back. Keep flinging it back out there until somebody catches it. Remember, you don't like every book you meet, so why would they? And just because you aren't drawn to certain books or types of books, it doesn't mean they're lousy books, *n'est-ce pas*?

Rejection, of course, is not easy to deal with. I gradually started to think of it more as an RSVP. In other words, I'd query an agent or editor and think *"Répondez s'il vous plaît,"* as in "respond, please." All you want is their response, preferably a "yes," but even if you get a rejection slip, at least you'll be further along in narrowing your search for an agent or editor who's a good match for you. Sometimes, it just isn't a good fit—for you, or for them.

One last tip: Pick up a copy of Andre Bernard's book *Rotten Rejections.* The author reprints numerous actual letters of rejection for what turned out to be literary masterpieces—letters that were sent to the likes of Joyce, Hemingway, Steinbeck, Whitman, and Flaubert, to name a few. If nothing else, it'll make you feel that you're in good company. And it will certainly remind you that agents, editors, and publishers are just as idiosyncratic and flawed as the rest of us.

Believe in your writing—and someday, perhaps sooner than you think, someone else will, too.

PART III

10 days to get out of your own way
the bi-vocal way

CHAPTER 10

what a difference a day makes:

how to choose the *write* response

If you ask me what I have come to do in the world,

I who am an artist,

I will reply: "I am here to live aloud."

—Emile Zola

On Success and Blunders

Now that you have learned the bi-vocal approach for tackling writer's block, let's jump into a Ten-Day Writing Plan to establish your preferred writing patterns through the bi-vocal approach. You'll learn how to relish the day's successes—and relinquish the day's blunders. As transitions from one day to the next, I've included brief anecdotes and words of encouragement to help you ease yourself through this ten-day process of establishing writing as an integral part of your life.

To Write or Not to Write

In my diary, as an adolescent, I developed my first bout of writer's block. Daunted by all those blank pages I'd face for 365 days, I wrote ahead for days at a time, sometimes for a month ahead, "Dear Diary, Today nothing very unusual happened"—except, of course, for the Beatles' birthdays, all four of which I noted in billboard-sized script as if they were international holidays. I suppose this was good—to make not writing a conscious choice—but it wasn't until many years later that I learned how to make writing a conscious choice.

That's why I've included this last chapter, so you can learn how to make writing—or not—a conscious choice every day. Although you may proceed to write no more than *"Today is Ringo's birthday!"* these pages are intended to help you avoid what is often called "page fright." Some days you may write a lot, other days nothing at all—but the important concept here is to make writing—or not—a conscious choice.

Paying Yourself First: Day 1

Now that you've mastered the bi-vocal approach, this chapter will help you assimilate it into your lifestyle over the next ten days.

For each day, you'll find a morning Task-Sprinting Chart (with consolidated suggestions from Chapters 1 through 5), as well as an optional Evening Check-in Chart. If possible, it's best to keep this book on your nightstand so your right brain has an instant visual reminder that you can choose to write—or not—over the next ten days.

Try to fill out your daily Task-Sprinting Chart upon awakening—before you're even out of bed. One of my favorite books by inspirational writer SARK is called *Change Your Life Without Getting Out of Bed* (a whimsical treatise on the art of napping)—and I'm convinced she's onto something. Staying in bed to complete your daily chart—even if it means waking up five minutes earlier—is also a way of *paying yourself first*. It's a clear message to your right brain that your writing needs are at the top of your priority list—even if it's just for a few minutes each day.

Part 1 of each Task-Sprinting Chart will offer you choices about how—and even whether—you'll write over the next ten days. Part 2 of each Task-Sprinting Chart offers you choices about mood, type of writing, and a brief bi-vocal internal dialogue to use *just before you begin your day's writing task*. You'll also find an optional, and I do mean optional, Evening Check-in Chart for each day, so you can note any progress, release the day's frustrations, and prepare your mind for the next day. Keep in mind that some days you'll probably feel more motivated than you do on other days—and that's okay. What counts is your ability to listen to *both* of your voices during the next ten days. Once you have established this as a habit, you can use the bi-vocal approach anywhere, anytime.

For example, let's say one of your goals is to outline a novel, and your chosen subtask for your Task-Sprinting Chart today is to decide on the classic three-act structure. Now, since you don't have a ten-hour distraction-free day for this task, your all-or-nothing right brain will want to take flight—and resort to random acts of chocolate, or whatever else you might find soothing. However, even if you don't write a word because you find yourself buried in a vat of butter pecan ice cream today, keep in mind you can do an Evening Check-in Chart tonight, switch over from your *flight mode* to your *write mode*, and fall asleep with that template brewing in your unconscious—better than a cup of espresso for tomorrow's wake-up call.

As you approach your Task-Sprinting Chart for Day 1, try to remember that these are choices, not commands. Choose one subtask from your Task-Shaping Chart in Chapter 2, and start there. You'll notice that these revised Task-Sprinting Charts have not only consolidated all the suggestions from Chapters 1 through 5, but they also provide a small block of white space—much less intimidating than an entire blank page—so you can jot a few thoughts about your day's planned writing episode, *if you want to*. On the days when you choose to jot a few notes in this optional space, you'll find that when you sit down later in the day for your sprint of writing, you'll already have a blip of creativity to track on your Muse's radar screen of productivity.

Even one small sprint of writing can make a difference in whether the Muse of Motivation will stop by. And don't forget to use your dopamine-craving right brain's Rewards List from Chapter 2 to give yourself credit for time served!

One last note: You may need to establish—and respect—your *prewriting routine*. For example, I like to have a cup of tea and breakfast, then read *some* of the newspaper, and then head up to my writing studio—or to the nearest café or diner. It's my way of easing myself into the writing process, and I no longer feel the least bit guilty about it!

Think about exactly what you need to do before you start writing, and allow yourself to have that whenever possible. For example, you might like to read fiction for twenty minutes, with a cup of coffee and a muffin, or you might like to go for a twenty-minute walk, then sit down with a glass of orange juice before you write. If it's a lunch-hour writing time, you might want to give yourself five minutes to eat something and just think about what you feel like writing today, before you actually begin to write. In other words, honor what your "reward-seeking" right brain *needs* before you start writing—remember, the right brain is basically about three years old, and, like any toddler, it will keep tugging on your shirt until you respond. (*Répondez s'il vous plaît?*)

Day 1

Dominant Hand

Today, I'll choose to be in: ___write mode ___flight mode.

Writing task:_____

Subtask for today:_____

Optional—Here's a few thoughts about my chosen writing task for later today:

_____

Later today,

I'll try task for:

__ 2 min. __ 5 min. __ 10 min. __ 15 min. __ 20 min. __ 30 min.

Time of day: _____ 1st choice _____ 2nd choice _____ 3rd choice

Place to write:

__ home __ office __ café/restaurant __ outdoors __ other

Writing tools:

__ favorite pen/pencil & paper __ computer __ crayons__ other

Reward time:

__ 2 min. __ 5 min. __ 10 min. __ 15 min. __ 20 min. __ 30 min.

What I'll do during my reward time:_____

Time of day for reward:

_____ 1st choice _____ 2nd choice _____ 3rd choice

Nondominant Hand

Comatose ....Overdrive

| Current Mood: | 0 | 1 | 2 | 3 | 4 | 5 | 6 | 7 | 8 | 9 | 10 |
| Desired Mood: | 0 | 1 | 2 | 3 | 4 | 5 | 6 | 7 | 8 | 9 | 10 |

Dominant Hand

Comatose ....Overdrive

| Current Mood: | 0 | 1 | 2 | 3 | 4 | 5 | 6 | 7 | 8 | 9 | 10 |
| Desired Mood: | 0 | 1 | 2 | 3 | 4 | 5 | 6 | 7 | 8 | 9 | 10 |

Today, I think I'll choose the mood/energy level selected by my: __ nondominant hand   __ dominant hand.
If I need to change mood:
raise energy by_____ lower tension by_____
Which type of writing I'd like to try right now:
__ read-writing __ cowriting __ rote-writing __ prewriting
__ writing __ rewriting

If I feel stuck: *What do I need to complete this subtask?* (Use nondominant hand.)

_____

How can I give this to myself? (Use dominant hand.)

_____

Now, I'll try task for:
__ 2 min. __ 5 min. __ 10 min. __ 15 min. __ 20 min. __ 30 min.
Actual time:
__ 2 min. __ 5 min. __ 10 min. __ 15 min. __ 20 min. __ 30 min.
Reward time:
__ 2 min. __ 5 min. __ 10 min. __ 15 min. __ 20 min. __ 30 min.

Right After Doing Some of the Subtask

What is my mood now?
Nondominant Hand

(Comatose) 0   1 2 3 4 5 6 7 8 9 10 (Overdrive)

Dominant Hand

(Comatose) 0   1 2 3 4 5 6 7 8 9 10 (Overdrive)

Do I want to sign on for another block of time right now?

___yes   ___no

If so, which type of writing can I do right now?

__ read-writing __ cowriting __ rote-writing __ prewriting

__ writing __ rewriting

Maybe I'll try another:

__ 2 min. __ 5 min. __ 10 min. __ 15 min. __ 20 min. __ 30 min.

Reward time:

__ 2 min. __ 5 min. __ 10 min. __ 15 min. __ 20 min. __ 30 min.

Evening Check-in Chart

Dominant Hand

Today, I___did/___did not do my chosen subtask.

As a result, I felt:_____.

The reason I___did/___did not do my subtask was because of:

____my mood ____other commitments ____other reasons (____).

Today, I___did/___did not give myself my reward time.

As a result, I felt:_____.

The reason I___did/___did not give myself reward time was because of:

___my mood ___other commitments ___other reasons (____).

When I tried to do today's subtask, I felt like I was in:

___write mode___flight mode.

Tomorrow, I'll choose to be in:___write mode ___flight mode.

What I'll need tomorrow to stay on track is:

Nondominant Hand:_____.

Dominant Hand:_____.

Finish each day and be done with it. . . .
Some blunders and absurdities no doubt crept in. . . .
Tomorrow is a new day; begin it well and serenely.
—Ralph Waldo Emerson

Day 2: Chaos Theory in Practice

Here you are on Day 2, and you're pretty sure the jig is up.

Why? Well, here are some possible reasons: It's only 8 A.M., and it's a snow day, and so you have a gaggle of delightful school-aged children underfoot, and maybe an electrical power surge has zapped your laptop, and your cat hurled a fur ball onto your manuscript, and your spouse's car broke down, and you forgot you must pay bills *today.*

You're thinking, this Ten-Day Writing Plan just isn't going to work. It's only Day 2, and life is simply getting in the way.

Does it have to? I've worked with clients who, in order to accommodate their twenty-minute writing plans, have decided to stop playing computer games at night, to sit in the parking lot after work and write before going home, to take a chunk of their lunch hour for writing, to write during their children's gymnastics class, etc. Maybe all you'll get to do today is jot down a few ideas for tomorrow—but that is one way of keeping your writing spirit alive.

So, call a tow truck, give the kids twenty minutes to set up a homemade tent—furnished, of course—in the living room, squeegee the fur ball off your manuscript, and handwrite whatever you can in those precious twenty minutes. You can pay the bills while the kids watch a video later, and your laptop can be assessed this evening. The point is, no matter how aggravating this day's circumstances may be, you still have: paper and pen, your writing hand, and a tiny degree of control over your time today. So, exercise them all: your hand, your pittance of control over your time, and your creativity.

If today were the designated day for your child's birthday party, you'd still find some way to celebrate it, right? So, do the same for your writing self—even if it's just for a few minutes today. Remember, *some* writing time is better than no writing time at all. And, once you have connected with your writing self for those precious few minutes, you'll feel a lot better about jumping into that tent with your kids to read stories and play games all day, and you won't even care that they broke your favorite vase while hauling objects to use as counterweights for the sheets and blankets covering their "three-room," split-level tent-house.

Here are your charts for Day 2.

Day 2

Dominant Hand

Today, I'll choose to be in: ___write mode ___flight mode.

Writing task:_____

Subtask for today:_____

Optional—Here's a few thoughts about my chosen writing task for later today:

_____

Later today,

I'll try task for:

__ 2 min. __5 min. __ 10 min. __ 15 min. __20 min. __30 min.

Time of day: ____ 1st choice ____ 2nd choice ____ 3rd choice

Place to write:

__ home __ office __ café/restaurant __ outdoors __ other

Writing tools:

__ favorite pen/pencil & paper __ computer __ crayons__ other

Reward time:

__ 2 min. __5 min. __ 10 min. __ 15 min. __20 min. __30 min.

What I'll do during my reward time:_____

Time of day for reward:

____ 1st choice ____ 2nd choice ____ 3rd choice

Nondominant Hand

Comatose...Overdrive

Current Mood: 0 1 2 3 4 5 6 7 8 9 10

Desired Mood: 0 1 2 3 4 5 6 7 8 9 10

Dominant Hand

Comatose...Overdrive

Current Mood: 0 1 2 3 4 5 6 7 8 9 10

Desired Mood: 0 1 2 3 4 5 6 7 8 9 10

Today, I think I'll choose the mood/energy level selected by my: __ nondominant hand   __ dominant hand.

If I need to change mood:

raise energy by_____ lower tension by_____

Which type of writing I'd like to try right now:

__ read-writing __ cowriting __ rote-writing __ prewriting

__ writing __ rewriting

If I feel stuck: *What do I need to complete this subtask?* (Use nondominant hand.)

_____

How can I give this to myself? (Use dominant hand.)

_____

Now, I'll try task for:

__ 2 min. __ 5 min. __ 10 min. __ 15 min. __ 20 min. __ 30 min.

Actual time:

__ 2 min. __ 5 min. __ 10 min. __ 15 min. __ 20 min. __ 30 min.

Reward time:

__ 2 min. __ 5 min. __ 10 min. __ 15 min. __ 20 min. __ 30 min.

Right After Doing Some of the Subtask

What is my mood now?

Nondominant Hand

(Comatose) 0   1 2 3 4 5 6 7 8 9 10 (Overdrive)

Dominant Hand

(Comatose) 0   1 2 3 4 5 6 7 8 9 10 (Overdrive)

Do I want to sign on for another block of time right now?

___ yes   ___ no

If so, which type of writing can I do right now?

__ read-writing __ cowriting __ rote-writing __ prewriting
__ writing __ rewriting

Maybe I'll try another:

__ 2 min. __ 5 min. __ 10 min. __ 15 min. __ 20 min. __ 30 min.

Reward time:

__ 2 min. __ 5 min. __ 10 min. __ 15 min. __ 20 min. __ 30 min.

Dominant Hand

Today, I___did/___did not do my chosen subtask.

As a result, I felt:_____.

The reason I___did/___did not do my subtask was because of:

___my mood ___other commitments ___other reasons (___).

Today, I___did/___did not give myself my reward time.

As a result, I felt:_____.

The reason I___did/___did not give myself reward time was because of:

___my mood ___other commitments ___other reasons (___).

When I tried to do today's subtask, I felt like I was in:

___write mode___flight mode.

Tomorrow, I'll choose to be in:___write mode ___flight mode.

What I'll need tomorrow to stay on track is:

Nondominant Hand:_____.

Dominant Hand:_____.

Finish each day and be done with it. . . .

Some blunders and absurdities no doubt crept in. . . .

Tomorrow is a new day; begin it well and serenely.

—Ralph Waldo Emerson

Day 3: Frustration or Incubation?

Hey, it's Day 3, and still your Great American Novel remains unwritten.

However, maybe you wrote a scene yesterday, and perhaps you'll write another scene today. They don't have to be complete, or perfect—just sketched onto the page. Stick figures, if that's all you can muster.

As a writer, I know how hard it is to be patient with the Muse. Like you, I want instant results. I have to remind myself that the creative process involves three stages: incubation, illumination, and elaboration. Like you, I'm not particularly fond of seeing my Muse trapped like a baby chick fighting its way out of its shell, but I know that incubation is necessary. That's why roughing it out on the page is just as important as the final manuscript. *Every step counts.*

On the other hand, all of this requires patience—the opposite of that familiar drive for instant gratification. Of course, you probably want to hold the finished writing project in your hands right now, preferably in a published format. But think about all the activities you've engaged in during your lifetime—such as graduating from high school, attaining a certification, or attending college—all the tasks that at the time seemed insurmountable, especially while you were having a life at the same time. Yet, somehow, your meandering path has brought you here, now. Perhaps it looks something like this:

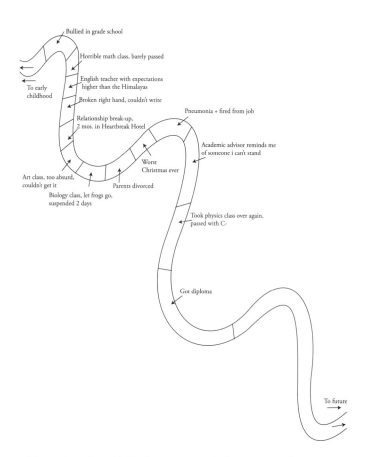

Bullied in grade school

Horrible math class, barely passed

English teacher with expectations higher than the Himalayas

To early childhood

Broken right hand, couldn't write

Relationship break-up, 2 mos. in Heartbreak Hotel

Pneumonia + fired from job

Academic advisor reminds me of someone i can't stand

Worst Christmas ever

Art class, too absurd, couldn't get it

Parents divorced

Biology class, let frogs go, suspended 2 days

Took physics class over again, passed with C-

Got diploma

To future

Now, in spite of all these ups and downs, you kept getting back up, and, step by step, inch by inch, somewhere in there you probably took every class you needed in order to get your high school diploma or GED, and perhaps even some other form of certification or college degree. Now, let's imagine how your path may look since you've started reading this book:

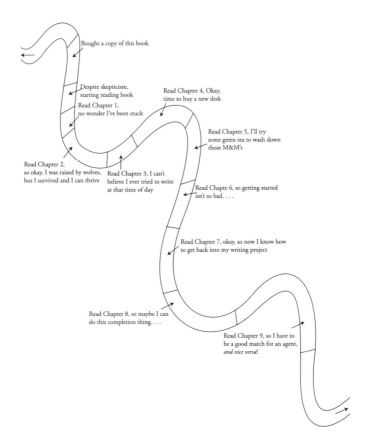

Now, let's say you complete the Ten-Day Plan in this chapter. Maybe it looks something like this:

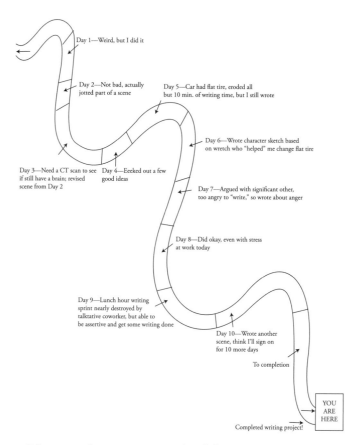

Day 1—Weird, but I did it

Day 2—Not bad, actually jotted part of a scene

Day 5—Car had flat tire, eroded all but 10 min. of writing time, but I still wrote

Day 6—Wrote character sketch based on wretch who "helped" me change flat tire

Day 3—Need a CT scan to see if still have a brain; revised scene from Day 2

Day 4—Eeeked out a few good ideas

Day 7—Argued with significant other, too angry to "write," so wrote about anger

Day 8—Did okay, even with stress at work today

Day 9—Lunch hour writing sprint nearly destroyed by talktative coworker, but able to be assertive and get some writing done

Day 10—Wrote another scene, think I'll sign on for 10 more days

To completion

YOU ARE HERE

Completed writing project!

Of course, this is just a sample of the many possibilities that may occur over the next ten days. Let's jump into Day 3 and see what happens!

Day 3

Dominant Hand

Today, I'll choose to be in: ___write mode ___flight mode.

Writing task:_____

Subtask for today:_____

Optional—Here's a few thoughts about my chosen writing task for later today:

_____

Later today,

I'll try task for:

__ 2 min. __ 5 min. __ 10 min. __ 15 min. __ 20 min. __ 30 min.

Time of day: ____ 1st choice ____ 2nd choice ____ 3rd choice

Place to write:

__ home __ office __ café/restaurant __ outdoors __ other

Writing tools:

__ favorite pen/pencil & paper __ computer __ crayons__ other

Reward time:

__ 2 min. __ 5 min. __ 10 min. __ 15 min. __ 20 min. __ 30 min.

What I'll do during my reward time:_____

Time of day for reward:

____ 1st choice ____ 2nd choice ____ 3rd choice

Nondominant Hand

Comatose ....Overdrive

Current Mood: 0 1 2 3 4 5 6 7 8 9 10

Desired Mood: 0 1 2 3 4 5 6 7 8 9 10

Dominant Hand

Comatose ....Overdrive

Current Mood: 0 1 2 3 4 5 6 7 8 9 10

Desired Mood: 0 1 2 3 4 5 6 7 8 9 10

Today, I think I'll choose the mood/energy level selected
by my: __ nondominant hand   __ dominant hand.

If I need to change mood:

*raise energy by*_____ *lower tension by*_____

Which type of writing I'd like to try right now:

__ read-writing __ cowriting __ rote-writing __ prewriting

__ writing __ rewriting

If I feel stuck: *What do I need to complete this subtask?*
(Use nondominant hand.)

_____

How can I give this to myself? (Use dominant hand.)

_____

Now, I'll try task for:

__ 2 min. __ 5 min. __ 10 min. __ 15 min. __ 20 min. __ 30 min.

Actual time:

__ 2 min. __ 5 min. __ 10 min. __ 15 min. __ 20 min. __ 30 min.

Reward time:

__ 2 min. __ 5 min. __ 10 min. __ 15 min. __ 20 min. __ 30 min.

Right After Doing Some of the Subtask

What is my mood now?

Nondominant Hand

(Comatose) 0   1 2 3 4 5 6 7 8 9 10 (Overdrive)

Dominant Hand

(Comatose) 0   1 2 3 4 5 6 7 8 9 10 (Overdrive)

Do I want to sign on for another block of time right now?

___ yes   ___no

If so, which type of writing can I do right now?

__ read-writing __ cowriting __ rote-writing __ prewriting

__ writing __ rewriting

Maybe I'll try another:

__ 2 min. __ 5 min. __ 10 min. __ 15 min. __ 20 min. __ 30 min.

Reward time:

__ 2 min. __ 5 min. __ 10 min. __ 15 min. __ 20 min. __ 30 min.

Evening Check-in Chart

Dominant Hand

Today, I___did/___did not do my chosen subtask.

As a result, I felt:_____.

The reason I___did/___did not do my subtask was because of:

____my mood ____other commitments ____other reasons (____).

Today, I___did/___did not give myself my reward time.

As a result, I felt:_____.

The reason I___did/___did not give myself reward time was because of:

___my mood ___other commitments ___other reasons (___).

When I tried to do today's subtask, I felt like I was in:

___write mode___flight mode.

Tomorrow, I'll choose to be in:___write mode ___flight mode.

What I'll need tomorrow to stay on track is:

Nondominant Hand:_____.

Dominant Hand:_____.

Finish each day and be done with it. . . .
Some blunders and absurdities no doubt crept in. . . .
Tomorrow is a new day; begin it well and serenely.
—Ralph Waldo Emerson

Day 4: Cleaning Countertops

Here you are, on Day 4, and no matter how well you've kept to your Ten-Day Writing Plan, somewhere in there you're probably harboring a fear that you won't get to keep this modicum of success. You may fear that you'll be tempted to go back to your chaos mode, rather than your relatively calm mode.

In the past, when I was faced with the write-or-flight response, I'd usually take flight immediately. I'd hurl myself into a flurry of meaningless activity—enough to keep three people busy for the entire day.

And what would I have at the end of the day? A headache, a stack of paid bills, an emptied voice mailbox, a sparkling kitchen countertop, a massive case of crankiness, and fourteen excuses for why I hadn't written.

You, too, can have a day just like that. But do you really want that? Think about making an active choice today: To do, or not to do—that is the question.

Unfortunately, sometimes we let other people answer that question for us. For example, I have worked with many clients whose significant others either actively discouraged or simply ignored the clients' dream of becoming a writer. One client was told by his wife that writing is "just a pipe dream"—and of course, given his already wavering self-esteem, this comment shut him down for months. He couldn't write a word. It was only after he realized that what counts is writing for himself—not for the approval of others—that he was able to write again.

With other writers, I have seen the toll that is taken by the sheer indifference of significant others. Psychologists call this "the null environment"—a situation where you are not actively being discouraged, but you're not getting any form of active encouragement, either. Being ignored can then "nullify" an individual's sense of self-worth, accomplishment, and ability to move forward in achieving a goal. The way out of this null environment is to create a new one—one in which you can feel good about your writing, regardless of your significant others' lack of appreciation.

Many nonwriters think that if you're not getting paid to write, then it's a waste of time. What they don't know is that, for writers, writing is a necessity, not a luxury. It's an expression of your deepest self through the prismed lens of creativity. Not writing feels like you're cut off from your *self*. That is why it may be helpful to connect with other writers. Many bookstores have free writer's groups where you can meet kindred spirits—who will obviously be more likely to pay attention to what—or whether—you're writing. You many even find other writers who are working with this book, and perhaps they are only at Day 2—but here you are at Day 4 already!

Day 4

Upon Awakening

Dominant Hand

Today, I'll choose to be in: ___write mode ___flight mode.

Writing task:_____

Subtask for today:_____

Optional—Here's a few thoughts about my chosen writing task for later today:

_____

Later today,

I'll try task for:

__ 2 min. __5 min. __ 10 min. __ 15 min. __ 20 min. __ 30 min.

Time of day: ____ 1st choice ____ 2nd choice ____ 3rd choice

Place to write:

__ home __ office __ café/restaurant __ outdoors __ other

Writing tools:

__ favorite pen/pencil & paper __ computer __ crayons__ other

Reward time:

__ 2 min. __ 5 min. __ 10 min. __ 15 min. __ 20 min. __ 30 min.

What I'll do during my reward time:_____

Time of day for reward:

_____ 1st choice _____ 2nd choice _____ 3rd choice

Just Before Trying the Subtask

Nondominant Hand

Comatose...Overdrive

Current Mood: 0   1   2   3   4   5   6   7   8   9   10

Desired Mood: 0   1   2   3   4   5   6   7   8   9   10

Dominant Hand

Comatose...Overdrive

Current Mood: 0   1   2   3   4   5   6   7   8   9   10

Desired Mood: 0   1   2   3   4   5   6   7   8   9   10

Today, I think I'll choose the mood/energy level selected
by my: __ nondominant hand   __ dominant hand.

If I need to change mood:

raise energy by_____ lower tension by_____

Which type of writing I'd like to try right now:

__ read-writing __ cowriting __ rote-writing __ prewriting
__ writing __ rewriting

If I feel stuck: *What do I need to complete this subtask?*
(Use nondominant hand.)

_____

How can I give this to myself? (Use dominant hand.)

_____

Now, I'll try task for:
__ 2 min. __ 5 min. __ 10 min. __ 15 min. __ 20 min. __ 30 min.
Actual time:
__ 2 min. __ 5 min. __ 10 min. __ 15 min. __ 20 min. __ 30 min.
Reward time:
__ 2 min. __ 5 min. __ 10 min. __ 15 min. __ 20 min. __ 30 min.

Right After Doing Some of the Subtask

What is my mood now?

Nondominant Hand

(Comatose) 0   1 2 3 4 5 6 7 8 9 10 (Overdrive)

Dominant Hand

(Comatose) 0   1 2 3 4 5 6 7 8 9 10 (Overdrive)

Do I want to sign on for another block of time right now?
___ yes   ___ no
If so, which type of writing can I do right now?
__ read-writing __ cowriting __ rote-writing __ prewriting
__ writing __ rewriting

Maybe I'll try another:
__ 2 min. __ 5 min. __ 10 min. __ 15 min. __ 20 min. __ 30 min.
Reward time:
__ 2 min. __ 5 min. __ 10 min. __ 15 min. __ 20 min. __ 30 min.

Dominant Hand

Today, I___did/___did not do my chosen subtask.

As a result, I felt:_____.

The reason I___did/___did not do my subtask was because of:

___my mood ___other commitments ___other reasons (___).

Today, I___did/___did not give myself my reward time.

As a result, I felt:_____.

The reason I___did/___did not give myself reward time was because of:

___my mood ___other commitments ___other reasons (___).

When I tried to do today's subtask, I felt like I was in:

___write mode___flight mode.

Tomorrow, I'll choose to be in:___write mode ___flight mode.

What I'll need tomorrow to stay on track is:

Nondominant Hand:_____.

Dominant Hand:_____.

Finish each day and be done with it. . . .

Some blunders and absurdities no doubt crept in. . . .

Tomorrow is a new day; begin it well and serenely.

—Ralph Waldo Emerson

Day 5: Chasing the Five O'clock Shadow

It's Day 5—you have arrived at the halfway point in your Ten-Day Writing Plan, so I think you deserve a story today. Let me entertain you.

I once spent an entire day avoiding the "completion" of my thesis for my M.A. in English. I say *completion*, with air quotes, because I'm talking about actually turning in a completed manuscript. All I had to do was deliver it to the dean of the graduate school, and poof—I would graduate with my master's degree in just a few weeks!

The manuscript—which my old perfectionistic self had worked on (and off) assiduously for five years—was due by 5 P.M. that day. What was my thought upon awakening that morning? *Hey, I've got all day—it's not due until five o'clock!*

And what did I do on that particular day? Why, I did laundry, of course, which at that time in my life meant hauling five loads in and out of the local Laundromat. Now, since I had *until five* to turn in my thesis, I decided to dump my clothes in the washers, and then scurry off to the post office, the bank, and the grocery store. Somewhere in there I got a flat tire, spent hours getting it fixed while my perishable groceries melted in the trunk, rushed back to shove my clothes in the dryers (all the while worrying that someone had made off with my best jeans), and barely made it to the dean's office. I catapulted myself into the building just moments before the clock struck five, only to find that the dean had apparently left a few minutes early, the office was closed, and there was no one to sign off on my manuscript.

After that, I pretty much turned into a pumpkin. Of course, no one came around the next day brandishing a glass slipper to prove that I'd actually *been* at the dean's office the night before. No, I was sitting back in my apartment, keenly aware that I wouldn't be graduating for another semester, but somehow still not quite believing the fact that time waits for no one.

Once again, I had unconsciously set up a whirlwind of chaos to conquer—hey, I was born and raised on it—but this time, I hadn't managed to conquer it. Like a child who engages in magical thinking (*I can do this, no matter what*), I thought that I'd set up a highly productive day, full of errands I'd put off in order to finish typing my thesis.

Now, I know better: First, turn in the thesis, then sneak off to a matinee, and if there's any time left over, stop off at the bank before having dinner out with friends to celebrate the completion of my manuscript. The moral of the story: Don't count your progress before you've hatched.

So, without further ado, assuming that you don't have to finish a master's thesis today, let's get on with Day 5 of your writing plan.

Day 5

Dominant Hand

Today, I'll choose to be in: ___write mode ___flight mode.

Writing task:_____

Subtask for today:_____

Optional—Here's a few thoughts about my chosen writing task for later today:

_____

Later today,

I'll try task for:

__ 2 min. __ 5 min. __ 10 min. __ 15 min. __ 20 min. __ 30 min.

Time of day: ____ 1st choice ____ 2nd choice ____ 3rd choice

Place to write:

__ home __ office __ café/restaurant __ outdoors __ other

Writing tools:

__ favorite pen/pencil & paper __ computer __ crayons__ other

Reward time:

__ 2 min. __ 5 min. __ 10 min. __ 15 min. __ 20 min. __ 30 min.

What I'll do during my reward time:_____

Time of day for reward:

____ 1st choice ____ 2nd choice ____ 3rd choice

Nondominant Hand

Comatose ....Overdrive

Current Mood: 0 1 2 3 4 5 6 7 8 9 10

Desired Mood: 0 1 2 3 4 5 6 7 8 9 10

Dominant Hand

Comatose ....Overdrive

Current Mood: 0 1 2 3 4 5 6 7 8 9 10

Desired Mood: 0 1 2 3 4 5 6 7 8 9 10

Today, I think I'll choose the mood/energy level selected
by my: __ nondominant hand   __ dominant hand.
If I need to change mood:
*raise energy by*_____ *lower tension by*_____
Which type of writing I'd like to try right now:
__ read-writing __ cowriting __ rote-writing __ prewriting
__ writing __ rewriting

If I feel stuck: *What do I need to complete this subtask?*
(Use nondominant hand.)

_____

How can I give this to myself? (Use dominant hand.)

_____

Now, I'll try task for:
__ 2 min. __ 5 min. __ 10 min. __ 15 min. __ 20 min. __ 30 min.
Actual time:
__ 2 min. __ 5 min. __ 10 min. __ 15 min. __ 20 min. __ 30 min.
Reward time:
__ 2 min. __ 5 min. __ 10 min. __ 15 min. __ 20 min. __ 30 min.

Right After Doing Some of the Subtask

What is my mood now?

Nondominant Hand

(Comatose) 0   1 2 3 4 5 6 7 8 9 10 (Overdrive)

Dominant Hand

(Comatose) 0   1 2 3 4 5 6 7 8 9 10 (Overdrive)

Do I want to sign on for another block of time right now?

___ yes   ___no

If so, which type of writing can I do right now?

__ read-writing __ cowriting __ rote-writing __ prewriting

__ writing __ rewriting

Maybe I'll try another:

__ 2 min. __ 5 min. __ 10 min. __ 15 min. __ 20 min. __ 30 min.

Reward time:

__ 2 min. __ 5 min. __ 10 min. __ 15 min. __ 20 min. __ 30 min.

Evening Check-in Chart

Dominant Hand

Today, I___did/___did not do my chosen subtask.

As a result, I felt:_____.

The reason I___did/___did not do my subtask was because of:

____my mood ____other commitments ____other reasons (____).

Today, I___did/___did not give myself my reward time.

As a result, I felt:_____.

The reason I___did/___did not give myself reward time was because of:

____my mood ____other commitments ____other reasons (____).

When I tried to do today's subtask, I felt like I was in:

___write mode___flight mode.

Tomorrow, I'll choose to be in:___write mode ___flight mode.

What I'll need tomorrow to stay on track is:

Nondominant Hand:_____.

Dominant Hand:_____.

Finish each day and be done with it. . . .
Some blunders and absurdities no doubt crept in. . . .
Tomorrow is a new day; begin it well and serenely.
—Ralph Waldo Emerson

Day 6: Lost and Found

You've come this far, and perhaps now you're wondering if you have written anything decent. Here's the answer: Probably.

Remember Anne Lamott's SFD concept? Unless you're that one-in-a-million writer who always functions in Dalai Lama mode, an SFD is probably what you've been eking out. On the other hand, a lousy first draft is all it takes to create—eventually—a polished manuscript.

So, for now, continue writing, but if you feel that you must re-read part of your manuscript in order to continue (issues regarding plot, order of ideas, etc.), that's a fine way to use your writing time today. Just try not to judge—or revise yet—what you've written so far, *unless that's all you can muster the energy for.*

To illustrate, let's take a look at a page from my SFD for this book.

Right now, I'm tired, and I'm in a pizzeria, awaiting take-out food, and I'm glad it won't be ready for another twenty minutes. Otherwise, would I be writing at all today? Probably not, considering the list of family-related errands and events on today's docket.

So this twenty-minute delay—thanks to a slow-to-heat brick oven—becomes my writing time for today. I wouldn't have had the "energy" to sit at my computer today, nor would I have allotted writing time today, given my schedule. It's often these unexpected, "found" chunks of time that result in some decent writing. As always, I had a few sheets of notebook paper and a pen tucked into my purse, so I dashed off these words you're reading right now.

See if you can take advantage of "found" time that comes your way today. Or, better yet, see if you can "lose" some time on another activity—even ten minutes—to get in touch with your writing self today.

Day 6

Upon Awakening
Dominant Hand
Today, I'll choose to be in: ___write mode   ___flight mode.
Writing task:_____
Subtask for today:_____
Optional—Here's a few thoughts about my chosen writing task for later today:
_____

Later today,
I'll try task for:
__ 2 min. __ 5 min. __ 10 min. __ 15 min. __ 20 min. __ 30 min.
Time of day: _____ 1st choice _____ 2nd choice _____ 3rd choice
Place to write:
__ home __ office __ café/restaurant __ outdoors __ other
Writing tools:
__ favorite pen/pencil & paper __ computer __ crayons__ other
Reward time:
__ 2 min. __ 5 min. __ 10 min. __ 15 min. __ 20 min. __ 30 min.
What I'll do during my reward time:_____
Time of day for reward:
_____ 1st choice _____ 2nd choice _____ 3rd choice

Nondominant Hand

Comatose...Overdrive

Current Mood: 0   1   2   3   4   5   6   7   8   9   10

Desired Mood: 0   1   2   3   4   5   6   7   8   9   10

Dominant Hand

Comatose...Overdrive

Current Mood: 0   1   2   3   4   5   6   7   8   9   10

Desired Mood: 0   1   2   3   4   5   6   7   8   9   10

Today, I think I'll choose the mood/energy level selected
by my: __ nondominant hand   __ dominant hand.
If I need to change mood:
raise energy by_____ lower tension by_____

Which type of writing I'd like to try right now:

__ read-writing __ cowriting __ rote-writing __ prewriting __ writing __ rewriting

If I feel stuck: *What do I need to complete this subtask?* (Use nondominant hand.)

_____

How can I give this to myself? (Use dominant hand.)

_____

Now, I'll try task for:

__ 2 min. __ 5 min. __ 10 min. __ 15 min. __ 20 min. __ 30 min.

Actual time:

__ 2 min. __ 5 min. __ 10 min. __ 15 min. __ 20 min. __ 30 min.

Reward time:

__ 2 min. __ 5 min. __ 10 min. __ 15 min. __ 20 min. __ 30 min.

Right After Doing Some of the Subtask

What is my mood now?

Nondominant Hand

(Comatose) 0   1 2 3 4 5 6 7 8 9 10 (Overdrive)

Dominant Hand

(Comatose) 0   1 2 3 4 5 6 7 8 9 10 (Overdrive)

Do I want to sign on for another block of time right now?

___ yes   ___ no

If so, which type of writing can I do right now?

__ read-writing __ cowriting __ rote-writing __ prewriting __ writing __ rewriting

Maybe I'll try another:
__ 2 min. __ 5 min. __ 10 min. __ 15 min. __ 20 min. __ 30 min.
Reward time:
__ 2 min. __ 5 min. __ 10 min. __ 15 min. __ 20 min. __ 30 min.

Evening Check-in Chart

Dominant Hand

Today, I___did/___did not do my chosen subtask.

As a result, I felt:_____.

The reason I___did/___did not do my subtask was because of:

____my mood ____other commitments ____other reasons (____).

Today, I___did/___did not give myself my reward time.

As a result, I felt:_____.

The reason I___did/___did not give myself reward time was because of:

____my mood ____other commitments ____other reasons (____).

When I tried to do today's subtask, I felt like I was in:

___write mode___flight mode.

Tomorrow, I'll choose to be in:___write mode ___flight mode.

What I'll need tomorrow to stay on track is:

Nondominant Hand:_____.

Dominant Hand:_____.

Finish each day and be done with it. . . .
Some blunders and absurdities no doubt crept in. . . .
Tomorrow is a new day; begin it well and serenely.
—Ralph Waldo Emerson

Day 7: "Found" Time, Again

Today, after attending a professional conference, I was awaiting my ride home from the hotel. Fortunately, the conference ended early, and I was unable to get in touch with the person who would pick me up. Once again, I had some "found" time.

Of course I had paper and pen, so I sat down and brainstormed this section. Here's a page from my SFD to prove it:

As I glanced out the hotel windows, I started thinking about some of the appallingly off-target rejection letters I'd seen in Andre Bernard's book *Rotten Rejections: A Literary Companion*—in particular, one publisher's rejection letter claiming that *The Diary of Anne Frank* wouldn't sell because no one would be interested in such a thing!

Then I thought, *what a great idea for a chunk of encouragement in the Ten-Day Writing Plan for my book!*

So, just in case you feel discouraged right about now, here are some reasons why, as writers, we all need to persevere—no matter what others may say. Because, quite frankly, they can be wrong.

For example, in *Rotten Rejections*, here is a quotation from one editor's absurd rejection letter to Rudyard Kipling: "I'm sorry, Mr. Kipling, but you just don't know how to use the English language."

Needless to say, this book hit a nerve among discouraged writers everywhere. Then, along with Bill Henderson, Andre Bernard went on to publish *Pushcart's Complete Rotten Reviews & Rejections*, which, for obvious reasons, became a bestseller in the *New York Times Book Review* and *Publishers Weekly*. Here are a few of the reasons why:

> Reviewer of Walt Whitman: "Whitman is as unacquainted with art as a hog is with mathematics."
>
> Editor, rejecting Samuel Beckett: "I wouldn't touch this with a barge pole."
>
> Reviewer of Emily Brontë's *Wuthering Heights*: "Here all the faults of *Jane Eyre* (by Charlotte Brontë) are magnified a thousand fold, and the only consolation which we have in reflecting upon it is that it will never be generally read."

Okay, had enough? Knowing the history of these famous authors, you can see that one editor's nightmare is another editor's dream! So keep on writing—someone out there will see the value of your book—you can target the most appropriate agents, editors, and publishers later.

First, and foremost, comes the writing.

Day 7

Upon Awakening

Dominant Hand

Today, I'll choose to be in: ___write mode   ___flight mode.

Writing task:_____

Subtask for today:_____

Optional—Here's a few thoughts about my chosen writing task for later today:

_____

Later today,

I'll try task for:

__ 2 min. __ 5 min. __ 10 min. __ 15 min. __ 20 min. __ 30 min.

Time of day: ____ 1st choice ____ 2nd choice ____ 3rd choice

Place to write:

__ home __ office __ café/restaurant __ outdoors __ other

Writing tools:

__ favorite pen/pencil & paper __ computer __ crayons__ other

Reward time:

__ 2 min. __ 5 min. __ 10 min. __ 15 min. __ 20 min. __ 30 min.

What I'll do during my reward time:_____

Time of day for reward:

____ 1st choice ____ 2nd choice ____ 3rd choice

Just Before Trying the Subtask

Nondominant Hand

Comatose ....Overdrive

Current Mood: 0 1 2 3 4 5 6 7 8 9 10

Desired Mood: 0 1 2 3 4 5 6 7 8 9 10

Dominant Hand

Comatose ....Overdrive

Current Mood: 0 1 2 3 4 5 6 7 8 9 10

Desired Mood: 0 1 2 3 4 5 6 7 8 9 10

Today, I think I'll choose the mood/energy level selected
by my: __ nondominant hand   __ dominant hand.

If I need to change mood:

*raise energy by*_____ *lower tension by*_____

Which type of writing I'd like to try right now:

__ read-writing __ cowriting __ rote-writing __ prewriting
__ writing __ rewriting

If I feel stuck: *What do I need to complete this subtask?*
(Use nondominant hand.)

_____

How can I give this to myself? (Use dominant hand.)

_____

Now, I'll try task for:

__ 2 min. __ 5 min. __ 10 min. __ 15 min. __ 20 min. __ 30 min.

Actual time:

__ 2 min. __ 5 min. __ 10 min. __ 15 min. __ 20 min. __ 30 min.

Reward time:

__ 2 min. __ 5 min. __ 10 min. __ 15 min. __ 20 min. __ 30 min.

Right After Doing Some of the Subtask

What is my mood now?

Nondominant Hand

(Comatose) 0   1 2 3 4 5 6 7 8 9 10 (Overdrive)

Dominant Hand

(Comatose) 0   1 2 3 4 5 6 7 8 9 10 (Overdrive)

Do I want to sign on for another block of time right now?

___ yes   ___ no

If so, which type of writing can I do right now?

__ read-writing __ cowriting __ rote-writing __ prewriting

__ writing __ rewriting

Maybe I'll try another:

__ 2 min. __ 5 min. __ 10 min. __ 15 min. __ 20 min. __ 30 min.

Reward time:

__ 2 min. __ 5 min. __ 10 min. __ 15 min. __ 20 min. __ 30 min.

Evening Check-in Chart

Dominant Hand

Today, I___did/___did not do my chosen subtask.

As a result, I felt:_____.

The reason I___did/___did not do my subtask was because of:

____my mood ____other commitments ____other reasons (____).

Today, I___did/___did not give myself my reward time.

As a result, I felt:_____.

The reason I___did/___did not give myself reward time was because of:

___my mood ___other commitments ___other reasons (___).

When I tried to do today's subtask, I felt like I was in:

___write mode___flight mode.

Tomorrow, I'll choose to be in:___write mode ___flight mode.

What I'll need tomorrow to stay on track is:

Nondominant Hand:_____.

Dominant Hand:_____.

> Finish each day and be done with it. . . .
> Some blunders and absurdities no doubt crept in. . . .
> Tomorrow is a new day; begin it well and serenely.
> —Ralph Waldo Emerson

Day 8: In Search of the Holy Green Grail

Okay, so you wake up today knowing this will be a tough one. You have your annual review at work, your child needs a lime green shirt for the school play tomorrow, your mother needs a ride to her physician's office, and today, if someone laments *there's nothing to eat around here*, it's true.

So, you visualize yourself getting pulverized in your annual review, then rushing out to annihilate your lunch hour/writing time in search of that lime green shirt, dashing back to work, leaving at five o'clock so you can deliver your mother to her M.D. by six, scurrying across the street to scavenge a gallon of milk, a box of Cheerios, a baked chicken, and a large dollop of someone else's idea of mashed potatoes, then ferrying your mother back home, and finally landing at your place by 7:30. If you're lucky.

Now, let's do an instant replay, with a more proactive spin. You see yourself going to work and tolerating your review, then calling a friend to see if he or she will query nearby department stores regarding your basic lime green kid's shirt, then calling ahead and paying for this Holy Grail by credit card, then spending fifteen minutes to pick it up, and the other forty-five minutes of your lunch hour grabbing a quick bite while you write at a local café. Now that you've connected with your writing self—in spite of the odds against you—you won't mind driving your mother to and from her appointment tonight, and you won't mind grabbing a quick dinner and breakfast supplies from the local grocer, either.

Not bad for a day in the life of a writer. No matter what chaos may be dumped on your day, you can still claim your right to write!

Day 8

Upon Awakening

Dominant Hand

Today, I'll choose to be in: ___write mode ___flight mode.

Writing task:_____

Subtask for today:_____

Optional—Here's a few thoughts about my chosen writing task for later today:

_____

Later today,

I'll try task for:

__ 2 min. __ 5 min. __ 10 min. __ 15 min. __ 20 min. __ 30 min.

Time of day: _____ 1st choice _____ 2nd choice _____ 3rd choice

Place to write:

__ home __ office __ café/restaurant __ outdoors __ other

Writing tools:

__ favorite pen/pencil & paper __ computer __ crayons__ other

Reward time:

__ 2 min. __ 5 min. __ 10 min. __ 15 min. __ 20 min. __ 30 min.

What I'll do during my reward time:_____

Time of day for reward:

_____ 1st choice _____ 2nd choice _____ 3rd choice

Just Before Trying the Subtask

Nondominant Hand

Comatose ....Overdrive

Current Mood: 0 1 2 3 4 5 6 7 8 9 10

Desired Mood: 0 1 2 3 4 5 6 7 8 9 10

Dominant Hand

Comatose ....Overdrive

Current Mood: 0 1 2 3 4 5 6 7 8 9 10

Desired Mood: 0 1 2 3 4 5 6 7 8 9 1 0

Today, I think I'll choose the mood/energy level selected by my: __ nondominant hand __ dominant hand.

If I need to change mood:

raise energy by_____ lower tension by_____

Which type of writing I'd like to try right now:

__ read-writing __ cowriting __ rote-writing __ prewriting
__ writing __ rewriting

If I feel stuck: *What do I need to complete this subtask?*
(Use nondominant hand.)

_____

How can I give this to myself? (Use dominant hand.)

_____

Now, I'll try task for:

__ 2 min. __ 5 min. __ 10 min. __ 15 min. __ 20 min. __ 30 min.
Actual time:

__ 2 min. __ 5 min. __ 10 min. __ 15 min. __ 20 min. __ 30 min.
Reward time:

__ 2 min. __ 5 min. __ 10 min. __ 15 min. __ 20 min. __ 30 min.

Right After Doing Some of the Subtask

What is my mood now?

Nondominant Hand

(Comatose) 0   1 2 3 4 5 6 7 8 9 10 (Overdrive)

Dominant Hand

(Comatose) 0   1 2 3 4 5 6 7 8 9 10 (Overdrive)

Do I want to sign on for another block of time right now?

___ yes   ___ no

If so, which type of writing can I do right now?

__ read-writing __ cowriting __ rote-writing __ prewriting
__ writing __ rewriting

Maybe I'll try another:
__ 2 min. __ 5 min. __ 10 min. __ 15 min. __ 20 min. __ 30 min.
Reward time:
__ 2 min. __ 5 min. __ 10 min. __ 15 min. __ 20 min. __ 30 min.

Evening Check-in Chart

Dominant Hand

Today, I___did/___did not do my chosen subtask.

As a result, I felt:_____.

The reason I___did/___did not do my subtask was because of:

____my mood ____other commitments ____other reasons (____).

Today, I___did/___did not give myself my reward time.

As a result, I felt:_____.

The reason I___did/___did not give myself reward time was because of:

____my mood ____other commitments ____other reasons (____).

When I tried to do today's subtask, I felt like I was in:

____write mode____flight mode.

Tomorrow, I'll choose to be in:____write mode ____flight mode.

What I'll need tomorrow to stay on track is:

Nondominant Hand:_____.

Dominant Hand:_____.

Finish each day and be done with it. . . .
Some blunders and absurdities no doubt crept in. . . .
Tomorrow is a new day; begin it well and serenely.
—Ralph Waldo Emerson

Day 9: With Time to Spare

You've made it this far, and no one has called from the Time Police to say that you've stolen back some writing moments from your allotted 168 hours per week. Dare you say, Hey, this pattern of writing just might work for me!

On the other hand, over these past nine days you no doubt have come across some of the issues that in the past have thwarted your writing process. We all have them—it's how we react to these roadblocks that makes a difference as to whether we'll actually write on any given day.

I learned a powerful lesson about this, many years ago. I was attending a writers' conference, and in one session hosted by two agents, the participants were asked to jot down—in just three minutes—everything that could possibly get in the way of them becoming bestselling writers.

Everyone scrambled to hit pen to page, as if this were some kind of a contest. The clock was ticking, and I sat there, staring at a blank page. *Did I have writer's block, again?! Why couldn't I think of anything?* I thought about some of my relationships—no, that wouldn't stop me from writing. I thought about my ability to make money—no, I'd always be able to afford pen and paper. I even thought, what if I were banished to the country formerly known as the U.S.S.R., where I'd be arrested for radical writing of any kind? Not likely.

Time's up, said the agents. I felt disappointed because I hadn't written a thing, and would have nothing to contribute to the discussion, in which, up to that point, I'd been quite active as a participant. The agents started asking people to raise their hands if they had jotted down ten or more items. No one raised a hand. Then the agents asked the same of anyone who'd jotted between five and ten items. Some hands went up. Then, the agents asked about those who'd written between one and five items. Most of the other hands went up. Finally, the agents asked if anyone had written "nothing." *Great, the shame of writer's block again,* I was thinking. Two people raised their hands: me and one other writer. The agents asked us to stand up and announce our names. Then, in a very calm voice, one agent said, "Remember these names, for they will be the ones you'll see on the bestseller list in years to come."

I was stunned, as was the rest of the class. I'm still stunned whenever I think about that moment. Now, here I am, many years later, writing a book about writer's block! Whether or not I'm ever on the bestseller list, I'm happy enough right now—because I have found a way to ensure that I can write whenever, and wherever, I find the time. (And, as you already know, I am always on the lookout for "found" time—which of course means I'm more likely to find some!)

So think about sidestepping your roadblocks to writing: Where there's a will, there's a writer. On to Day 9!

Day 9

Dominant Hand

Today, I'll choose to be in: __write mode __flight mode.

Writing task:_____

Subtask for today:_____

Optional—Here's a few thoughts about my chosen writing task for later today:

_____

Later today,

I'll try task for:

__ 2 min. __ 5 min. __ 10 min. __ 15 min. __ 20 min. __ 30 min.

Time of day: ____ 1st choice ____ 2nd choice ____ 3rd choice

Place to write:

__ home __ office __ café/restaurant __ outdoors __ other

Writing tools:

__ favorite pen/pencil & paper __ computer __ crayons__ other

Reward time:

__ 2 min. __ 5 min. __ 10 min. __ 15 min. __ 20 min. __ 30 min.

What I'll do during my reward time:_____

Time of day for reward:

____ 1st choice ____ 2nd choice ____ 3rd choice

Nondominant Hand

Comatose . . . . .Overdrive

Current Mood: 0 1 2 3 4 5 6 7 8 9 10

Desired Mood: 0 1 2 3 4 5 6 7 8 9 10

Dominant Hand

Comatose . . . . .Overdrive

Current Mood: 0 1 2 3 4 5 6 7 8 9 10

Desired Mood: 0 1 2 3 4 5 6 7 8 9 10

Today, I think I'll choose the mood/energy level selected by my: __ nondominant hand   __ dominant hand.

If I need to change mood:

*raise energy by*_____ *lower tension by*_____

Which type of writing I'd like to try right now:

__ read-writing __ cowriting __ rote-writing __ prewriting

__ writing __ rewriting

If I feel stuck: *What do I need to complete this subtask?* (Use nondominant hand.)

_____

How can I give this to myself? (Use dominant hand.)

_____

Now, I'll try task for:

__ 2 min. __ 5 min. __ 10 min. __ 15 min. __ 20 min. __ 30 min.

Actual time:

__ 2 min. __ 5 min. __ 10 min. __ 15 min. __ 20 min. __ 30 min.

Reward time:

__ 2 min. __ 5 min. __ 10 min. __ 15 min. __ 20 min. __ 30 min.

What is my mood now?

Nondominant Hand

(Comatose) 0   1 2 3 4 5 6 7 8 9 10 (Overdrive)

Dominant Hand

(Comatose) 0   1 2 3 4 5 6 7 8 9 10 (Overdrive)

Do I want to sign on for another block of time right now?

___ yes   ___no

If so, which type of writing can I do right now?

__ read-writing __ cowriting __ rote-writing __ prewriting

__ writing __ rewriting

Maybe I'll try another:

__ 2 min. __ 5 min. __ 10 min. __ 15 min. __ 20 min. __ 30 min.

Reward time:

__ 2 min. __ 5 min. __ 10 min. __ 15 min. __ 20 min. __ 30 min.

Evening Check-in Chart

Dominant Hand

Today, I___did/___did not do my chosen subtask.

As a result, I felt:_____.

The reason I___did/___did not do my subtask was because of:

____my mood ____other commitments ____other reasons (____).

Today, I___did/___did not give myself my reward time.

As a result, I felt:_____.

The reason I___did/___did not give myself reward time was because of:

___my mood ___other commitments ___other reasons (___).

When I tried to do today's subtask, I felt like I was in:

___write mode___flight mode.

Tomorrow, I'll choose to be in:___write mode ___flight mode.

What I'll need tomorrow to stay on track is:

Nondominant Hand:_____.

Dominant Hand:_____.

Finish each day and be done with it. . . .
Some blunders and absurdities no doubt crept in. . . .
Tomorrow is a new day; begin it well and serenely.
—Ralph Waldo Emerson

Day 10: A Patch a Day Keeps the Blockage Away

Congratulations—you've made it to Day 10.

Does this mean you have developed a perfectly synchronized and highly productive writing life?

No.

Does this mean you care enough about your-self-as-writer to try to establish a reasonable expectation that you *can* write in small chunks of time?

Yes.

Believe it or not, that's how I got this book done. Right now, I'm back at the local diner, where, of course, I have long since surpassed the state of being a mere "regular," and have no doubt been dubbed "that woman with the big briefcase who sits there forever but at least she tips." I'm writing the last portion of this book between bites of chicken tenders (read: dopamine) and sips of tea (read: dopamine).

Like you, I've learned that *some* writing time is better than no writing time at all. Sure, I'd prefer a Big Block of Time in a luxury hotel suite with plenty of room service, but then, I'd probably be overwhelmed with the weight of expectations regarding that Big Block of Time, and I'd miss my family and friends, and I'd feel guilty if I didn't spend every minute writing—heaven forbid I might need some down time to allow for creative incubation.

The truth is, whether I'm writing fiction or nonfiction, I almost prefer these stolen chunks of time over an extended block of time. I recall writing my first novel in long blocks of time, accompanied by much angst and wringing of hands; on the other hand, I recall writing my second novel mostly by grabbing twenty-minute blocks of time at a café near my office, accompanied by much delight in what I could accomplish by writing just one small scene at a time. Sure, there are times when I need—and therefore set up—a large portion of time to synthesize what I've written through this patchwork quilt method of writing. Somewhere in there, I'll jot down an outline or a plot line with the classic three-act structure. But, I am also keenly aware that a patchwork quilt isn't usually sewn together in one sitting—at least not by one person!

The point is, by the time I am able to carve out a large portion of time, I have eked out some good pieces of writing. I have also had the additional benefit of *time between writing periods*, so that I can now review my work with a more neutral editor's eye, rather than the instant-gratification-oriented writer's eye (translation: "I just wrote it, so of course it's good"). And, because I have some chunks of completed writing to work with, I'm not intimidated by the blank page or the blinking cursor!

So, without further ado, let's create another "patch" of writing for your quilt of creativity today.

Day 10

Upon Awakening

Dominant Hand

Today, I'll choose to be in: ___write mode ___flight mode.

Writing task:_____

Subtask for today:_____

Optional—Here's a few thoughts about my chosen writing task for later today:

_____

Later today,

I'll try task for:

__ 2 min. __ 5 min. __ 10 min. __ 15 min. __ 20 min. __ 30 min.

Time of day: ____ 1st choice ____ 2nd choice ____ 3rd choice

Place to write:

__ home __ office __ café/restaurant __ outdoors __ other

Writing tools:

__ favorite pen/pencil & paper __ computer __ crayons__ other

Reward time:

__ 2 min. __ 5 min. __ 10 min. __ 15 min. __ 20 min. __ 30 min.

What I'll do during my reward time:_____

Time of day for reward:

____ 1st choice ____ 2nd choice ____ 3rd choice

Just Before Trying the Subtask

Nondominant Hand

Comatose ....Overdrive

Current Mood: 0 1 2 3 4 5 6 7 8 9 10

Desired Mood: 0 1 2 3 4 5 6 7 8 9 10

Dominant Hand

Comatose ....Overdrive

Current Mood: 0 1 2 3 4 5 6 7 8 9 10

Desired Mood: 0 1 2 3 4 5 6 7 8 9 10

Today, I think I'll choose the mood/energy level selected
by my: __ nondominant hand   __ dominant hand.
If I need to change mood:
raise energy by_____ lower tension by_____
Which type of writing I'd like to try right now:
__ read-writing __ cowriting __ rote-writing __ prewriting
__ writing __ rewriting

If I feel stuck: *What do I need to complete this subtask?*
(Use nondominant hand.)

_____

How can I give this to myself? (Use dominant hand.)

_____

Now, I'll try task for:
__ 2 min. __ 5 min. __ 10 min. __ 15 min. __ 20 min. __ 30 min.
Actual time:
__ 2 min. __ 5 min. __ 10 min. __ 15 min. __ 20 min. __ 30 min.
Reward time:
__ 2 min. __ 5 min. __ 10 min. __ 15 min. __ 20 min. __ 30 min.

Right After Doing Some of the Subtask

What is my mood now?

Nondominant Hand

(Comatose) 0   1 2 3 4 5 6 7 8 9 10 (Overdrive)

Dominant Hand

(Comatose) 0   1 2 3 4 5 6 7 8 9 10 (Overdrive)

Do I want to sign on for another block of time right now?

___ yes   ___no

If so, which type of writing can I do right now?

__ read-writing __ cowriting __ rote-writing __ prewriting

__ writing __ rewriting

Maybe I'll try another:

__ 2 min. __ 5 min. __ 10 min. __ 15 min. __ 20 min. __ 30 min.

Reward time:

__ 2 min. __ 5 min. __ 10 min. __ 15 min. __ 20 min. __ 30 min.

Evening Check-in Chart

Dominant Hand

Today, I___did/___did not do my chosen subtask.

As a result, I felt:_____.

The reason I___did/___did not do my subtask was because of:

____my mood ____other commitments ____other reasons (____).

Today, I___did/___did not give myself my reward time.

As a result, I felt:_____.

The reason I___did/___did not give myself reward time was
because of:

____my mood ____other commitments ____other reasons (____).

When I tried to do today's subtask, I felt like I was in:

___write mode___flight mode.

Tomorrow, I'll choose to be in:___write mode ___flight mode.

What I'll need tomorrow to stay on track is:

Nondominant Hand:_____.

Dominant Hand:_____.

Finish each day and be done with it. . . .
Some blunders and absurdities no doubt crept in. . . .
Tomorrow is a new day; begin it well and serenely.
—Ralph Waldo Emerson

Epilogue: And Now a Few Words from Your Inner Sponsor

Well, ten days have come and gone, and whether or not they have been the most prolific ten days in your life, you have claimed your right to write!

As you move beyond these first ten days, ask a friend to check in with you as you proceed in your writing plan. Be sure that it's someone who will actually care whether or not you've claimed your right to write on any given day. If you feel that you still need the structure of your Ten-Day Writing Plan, feel free to use the summary charts in the appendices of this book—or simply re-create the ten-day plan over and over again.

What's important to remember is this: You can choose to do this, to make writing an integral part—however small—of your daily life. It's a way of honoring the spirit within you—that creative self who's been waiting so long for an invitation to come out and play.

Only you can offer that invitation.

And only you can ever know just how essential that personal invitation really is.

So—invite, invite, invite. Take a few minutes—or even hours—back from the rest of your life, every week. If you don't, something may be left unsaid.

And that, my friend, would be denying part of your essential destiny.

So, on that note, I will leave you with my favorite comment about destiny, from Kurt Vonnegut's novel *Slapstick*. As the author muses about why the comedy of Laurel and Hardy held such a universal appeal—particularly during the Great Depression and World War II—he writes about their tenacity in overcoming the most impossible of odds. Sure, they find that a monkey with a wind-up organ is a great way to make money as street vendors during a time when there were no jobs available. But the monkey runs away. So, they decide to play the organ themselves, and they place their hats once again on the sidewalk for passersby to drop in coins of appreciation for this unexpected sidewalk entertainment. When the leg on the organ breaks, they find a way to prop it up. Finally, the organ rolls into the street, and, filled with hope, the two men rush out to reclaim it, only to be thwarted by a car that flattens the organ into unrecognizable rubble.

And here is what Vonnegut has to say about the unswerving tenacity of these two men: "The fundamental joke with Laurel and Hardy, it seems to me, was that they did their best with every test. They never failed to bargain in good faith with their destinies." So, the next time your writing time gets squashed into an unrecognizable pile of rubble (a flat tire, an unexpected meeting, the flu, twenty-five unnecessary phone calls, you name it), remember that you, too, can bargain in good faith with destiny.

The choice is yours. And so is your destiny.

Appendices: Your "To-Go" Order of Motivation

Appendix 1—To-Do (or Not-To-Do) List

Task:___

Estimated Time	Subtask	Actual Time	Reward Time
_____	1. _____	____	____
_____	2. _____	____	____
_____	3. _____	____	____
_____	4. _____	____	____
_____	5. _____	____	____
_____	6. _____	____	____
_____	7. _____	____	____
_____	8. _____	____	____
_____	9. _____	____	____
_____	10. _____	____	____

Appendix 2—Task-Sprinting Chart

Task-Sprinting Chart

Task: _____

Nondominant Hand

Comatose................................ Overdrive

Current Mood: 0 1 2 3 4 5 6 7 8 9 10

Desired Mood: 0 1 2 3 4 5 6 7 8 9 10

Dominant Hand
Dominant Hand

Comatose................................ Overdrive

Current Mood: 0 1 2 3 4 5 6 7 8 9 10

Desired Mood: 0 1 2 3 4 5 6 7 8 9 10

Today, I think I'll choose the energy level selected by my
___nondominant brain   ___dominant brain.

To Change Mood: *raise energy by___ lower tension by _____*
I'll try task for:

__ 2 min. __ 5 min. __ 10 min. __ 15 min. __ 20 min. __ 30 min.

Actual time:

__ 2 min. __ 5 min. __ 10 min. __ 15 min. __ 20 min. __ 30 min.

Reward time:

__ 2 min. __ 5 min. __ 10 min. __ 15 min. __ 20 min. __ 30 min.

Appendix 3—Parallel Monologue Chart

Dominant Hand
When I think about being a writer, I feel:_____.

Nondominant Hand
When I think about being a writer, I feel:_____.

Appendix 4—Interior Dialogue Chart

Interior Dialogue

Dominant hand: What do you need right now?

Nondominant hand: _____

Dominant hand: What would you need to be able to do this writing task?

Nondominant hand: _____

Dominant hand: Let me see if I can find a way to get you what you need. Maybe we can_____ , or we could_____ , either now or after twenty minutes of writing. Would that help?

Nondominant hand: _____

Dominant hand: Okay, then, are you ready to try this for a few minutes?

Nondominant hand: _____

Appendix 5—Write-or-Flight Chart

	Flight	Write
Choices	**Half-Brained Approach**	**Whole-Brain Approach**
Goal	*Write novel*	Write a chapter—any chapter
Subgoal	*Do it all*	Write one scene—any scene
Subtask	*What's that?*	Spend 20 minutes writing dialogue (or exposition about the setting) for any scene
Date	*Never*	Tuesday, 2:00–2:20
Reward	Only kick self while down 10 times instead of 30 times	20 minutes of reward time (reading, phone calls, checking e-mail, time toward going to a movie)
Current mood	Tense-tired	Tense-tired
Desired mood	Tense-energy	Calm-energy
Raise energy	Fry brains with coffee; solidify blood with nicotine; coagulate arteries with box of chocolates	Cup of green tea with dark chocolate bar; 5-min. brisk walk (indoors or outdoors); 20 rapid, deep breaths
Reduce tension	Inhale can of Pringles; hook up IV of Häagen-Dazs; scarf down pizza with a beer chaser	Cup of chamomile tea; 5 shoulder scrunches; 20 slow, deep breaths

Bibliography

Ainsworth, M.D., and C. Eichberg, "Effects on Infant-Mother Attachment of Mother's Unresolved Loss of an Attachment Figure, or Other Traumatic Experience," in *Attachment Across the Life Cycle,* eds. Colin Parkes, Joan Stevenson-Hinde, and Peter Marris (New York: Routledge, 1991), pp. 160–183.

Balch, James F., and Phyllis A. Balch. *Prescription for Nutritional Healing: A Practical A–Z Reference to Drug-Free Remedies Using Vitamins, Minerals, Herbs, & Food Supplements* (Garden City Park, NY: Avery Publishing Group, 1990).

Bernard, Andre. *Rotten Rejections: A Literary Companion.* (Wainscott, NY: Pushcart Press, 1990).

Borysenko, Joan. *Fire in the Soul: A New Psychology of Spiritual Optimism* (New York: Warner Books, 1993).

Bradbury, Ray. *Zen in the Art of Writing* (Santa Barbara: Capra Press, 1990).

Bradshaw, John. *Homecoming* (New York: Bantam, 1990).

Bremner, J. D., et al. "Magnetic Resonance Imaging-Based Measurement of Hippocampal Volume in Posttraumatic Stress Disorder Related to Childhood Physical and Sexual Abuse—A Preliminary Report." *Biological Psychiatry* 41 (1997): pp. 23–32.

Brewin, Chris R., and Hayley Lennard. "Effects of Mode of Writing on Emotional Narratives." *Journal of Traumatic Stress* 12, no. 2 (April 1999): pp. 355–361.

Browne, Renni, and Dave King. *Self-Editing for Fiction Writers: How to Edit Yourself into Print* (New York: HarperCollins, 1993).

Capacchione, Lucia. *The Power of Your Other Hand: A Course in Channeling the Inner Wisdom of the Right Brain* (Portland: Borgo Press, 1988).

Chopra, Deepak. *Perfect Health: The Complete Mind/Body Guide* (New York: Harmony Books, 1991).

De Bellis, Michael D., Matcheri S. Keshaven, Heather Shifflett, Satish Iyengar et al. "Brain Structures in Pediatric Maltreatment-Related Posttraumatic Stress Disorder: A Sociodemographically Matched Study." *Biological Psychiatry* 52, no. 11 (December 2002): pp. 1066–1078.

Ferrari, Joseph, Judith Johnson, and William McCown. *Procrastination and Task Avoidance: Theory, Research, and Treatment* (New York: Plenum Press, 1995).

Gil, Eliana. *Outgrowing the Pain: A Book for and about Adults Abused as Children* (New York: Dell, 1983).

Heim, Christine, Gunther Meinlschmidt, and Charles B. Nemeroff. "Neurobiology of Early-Life Stress." *Psychiatric Annals* 33, no. 1 (January 2000): pp. 18–26.

Henderson, Bill, and Andre Bernard, eds. *Pushcart's Complete Rotten Reviews & Rejections* (New York: Pushcart Press, 1998).

Herman, Jeff. *Guide to Book Publishers, Editors, and Literary Agents 2004.* (Waukesha, WI: Kalmbach Publishing Co., 2003).

Howard, Pierce. *The Owner's Manual for the Brain: Everyday Applications from Mind-Brain Research.* 2nd ed. (Austin: Bard Press, 2000).

Iaccino, James. *Left Brain-Right Brain Differences: Inquiries, Evidence, and New Approaches* (Hillsdale, NJ: Lawrence Erlbaum Associates, 1993).

Johnson, Stephen M. *Character Styles* (New York: W. W. Norton, 1994).

Joseph, R. *The Right Brain and the Unconscious: Discovering the Stranger Within* (New York: Plenum Press, 1992).

King, Stephen. *On Writing* (New York: Pocket Books, 2002).

Kitterle, Frederick. *Hemispheric Communication: Mechanisms and Models* (Hillsdale, NJ: Lawrence Erlbaum Associates, 1995).

Klauser, Henriette Anne. *Writing on Both Sides of the Brain.* (New York: HarperSanFrancisco, 1987).

Kranowitz, Carol. *The Out-of-Sync Child: Recognizing and Coping with Sensory Processing Disorder* (New York: Perigee, 1998).

Lamott, Anne. *Bird by Bird: Some Instructions on Writing and Life* (New York: Pantheon Books, 1994).

Lehmkuhl, Dorothy, and Dolores Cotter Lamping. *Organizing for the Creative Person: Right-Brain Styles for Conquering Clutter, Mastering Time, and Reaching Your Goals* (New York: Crown Publishers, 1993).

Lepore, Stephen, and Joshua Smyth. *The Writing Cure: How Expressive Writing Promotes Health and Emotional Well-Being* (Washington, DC: American Psychological Association, 2002).

Lindfors, Petra, and Ulf Lundberg. "Is Low Cortisol Release an Indicator of Positive Health?" *Stress and Health: Journal of the International Society for the Investigation of Stress* 18, no. 4 (October 2002): pp. 153–160.

Lukeman, Noah. *The First Five Pages: A Writer's Guide to Staying Out of the Rejection Pile* (New York: Fireside, 2000).

———. *The Plot Thickens: 8 Ways to Bring Fiction to Life* (New York: St. Martin's Press, 2002).

Lundberg, U., and M. Frankenhauser. "Pituitary-Adrenal and Sympathetic-Adrenal Correlates of Distress and Effort." *Journal of Psychosomatic Research* 24 (1980): pp. 125–130.

Lyon, Elizabeth. *Nonfiction Book Proposals Anybody Can Write: How to Get a Contract and Advance <u>Before</u> Writing Your Book.* Rev. ed. (New York: Perigee, 2000).

Main, M., and R. Goldwyn. "Predicting Rejection of Her Infant from Mother's Representation of Her Own Experiences: A Preliminary Report." *Child Abuse & Neglect* 8 (1984): pp. 203–217.

Maté, Gabor. *Scattered: How Attention Deficit Disorder Originates and What You Can Do about It* (New York: Plume, 1999).

Mayell, Mark. *Natural Energy: A Consumer's Guide to Legal, Mind-Altering and Mood-Brightening Herbs and Supplements* (New York: Three Rivers Press, 1998).

McEwen, Bruce S. "The Neurobiology and Neuroendocrinology of Stress: Implications for Posttraumatic Stress Disorder from a Basic Science Perspective." *Psychiatric Clinics of North America* 25, no. 2 (June 2002): pp. 469–494.

McFarlane, Alexander C., Rachel Yehuda, and C. Richard Clark. "Biologic Models of Traumatic Memories and Posttraumatic Stress Disorder: The Role of Neural Networks." *Psychiatric Clinics of North America* 25, no. 2 (June 2002): pp. 253–270.

Moore, B. "Cortisol, Stress, and Depression." *British Journal of Psychiatry* 181, no. 4 (October 2002): p. 348.

Murphy, Kevin R. *Out of the Fog: Treatment Options and Coping Strategies for Adult Attention Deficit Disorder* (New York: Hyperion, 1995).

Newman, M., and B. Berkowitz. *How to Take Charge of Your Life* (New York: Bantam, 1977).

Norden, Michael J. *Beyond Prozac: Antidotes for Modern Times* (New York: ReganBooks, 1996).

Parkes, Colin, Joan Stevenson-Hinde, and Peter Marris Peter. *Attachment Across the Life Cycle* (New York: Routledge, 1991).

Passons, William R. *Gestalt Approaches to Counseling* (New York: Holt, Rinehart, and Winston, 1975).

Pearson, Dirk, and S. Shaw. *Life Extension: A Practical Scientific Approach* (New York: Warner Books, 1982).

Peeke, Pamela. *Fight Fat after Forty: The Revolutionary Three-Pronged Approach That Will Break Your Stress-Fat Cycle and Make You Healthy, Fit, and Trim for Life* (New York: Viking, 2000).

Pennebaker, James. *Opening Up: The Healing Power of Confiding in Others* (New York: Avon Books, 1990).

———. *Writing to Heal: A Guided Journal for Recovering from Trauma and Emotional Upheaval* (Oakland, CA: New Harbinger Publications, 2004).

Peterson, Karen. *The Tomorrow Trap: Unlocking the Secrets of the Procrastination-Protection Syndrome* (Deerfield Beach, FL: Health Communications, 1996).

Phelan, Thomas. *1-2-3 Magic: Effective Discipline for Children 2–12.* 3rd ed. (Glen Ellyn, IL: Parentmagic, Inc., 2003).

Plimpton, George. *The Writer's Chapbook: A Compendium of Fact, Opinion, Wit, and Advice from the 20ᵗʰ Century's Preeminent Writers*. (New York: Viking, 1989).

Power, T. G., and M. L. Chapieski. "Childrearing and Impulse Control in Toddlers: A Naturalistic Investigation." *Developmental Psychology* 22 (1986): pp. 271–275.

Rodale, J. I. *The Synonym Finder* (New York: Warner Books, 1978).

Rogers, Bruce Holland. *Word Work*: *Surviving and Thriving as a Writer* (Montpelier, VT: Invisible Cities Press, 2002).

SARK. *Change Your Life Without Getting Out of Bed: The Ultimate Nap Book* (New York: Fireside, 1999).

Schiffer, Fredric. *Of Two Minds: The Revolutionary Science of Dual-Brain Psychology* (New York: Free Press, 1998).

Schore, Allan. *Affect Dysregulation and Disorders of the Self* (New York: W. W. Norton, 2003).

———. *Affect Regulation and the Origin of the Self: The Neurobiology of Emotional Development* (Hillsdale, NJ: Lawrence Erlbaum Associates, 1994).

———. *Affect Regulation and the Repair of the Self* (New York: W. W. Norton, 2003).

Schwartz, Jeffrey M. *Brain Lock: Free Yourself from Obsessive-Compulsive Behavior* (New York: ReganBooks/HarperCollins, 1996).

Shapiro, Francine, and Margot Forrest. *EMDR: The Breakthrough Therapy for Overcoming Anxiety, Stress, and Trauma* (New York: Basic Books, 1997).

Stark, Amy. *Because I Said So: Recognize the Influence of Childhood Dynamics on Office Politics and Take Charge of Your Career* (New York: Pharos Books, 1992).

Starkman, Monica N., Bruno Giordani, Stephen Gebarski, and David E. Schteingart. "Improvement in Learning Associated with Increase in Hippocampal Formation Volume." *Biological Psychiatry* 53, no. 3 (February 2003): pp. 233–238.

Storr, Anthony. *Solitude: A Return to the Self* (New York: Free Press, 1988).

Teicher, Martin H., Susan L. Andersen, Ann Polcari, Carl M. Anderson et al. "Developmental Neurobiology of Childhood Stress and Trauma." *Psychiatric Clinics of North America* 25, no. 2 (June 2002): pp. 397–426.

Teicher, Martin. "Scars That Won't Heal: The Neurobiology of Child Abuse; Maltreatment at an Early Age Can Have Enduring Negative Effects on a Child's Brain Development and Function." *Scientific America* 286, no. 13 (March 2002): pp. 68-75.

Tennes, K., K. Downey, K., and A. Vernadakis. "Urinary Cortisol Excretion Rates and Anxiety in Normal 1-Year-Old Infants." *Psychosomatic Medicine* 39 (1977): pp. 1178–1187.

Thayer, Robert. *Calm Energy: How People Regulate Mood with Food and Exercise* (New York: Oxford University Press, 2001).

————. *The Origin of Everyday Moods: Managing Energy, Tension, and Stress* (New York: Oxford University Press, 1996).

Trad, P. V. *Infant Depression* (New York: Springer-Verlag, 1986).

Tulkin, S. R., and J. Kagan. "Mother-Infant Interaction in the First Year of Life." *Child Development* 43 (1972): pp. 31–42.

van der Kolk, Bessell. "Integrating Basic Neuroscience and Clinical Realities: A Comprehensive Treatment Approach to Complex Post-Traumatic Stress Disorders." Paper presented at conference on Psychological Trauma: Maturational Processes and Therapeutic Interventions, Boston University School of Medicine, Division of Psychiatry, March 10–11, 2000, Boston, MA.

van der Kolk, Bessell, O. van der Hart, and C. Marmar. "Dissociation and Information Processing in Posttraumatic Stress Disorder," *Traumatic Stress* (New York: The Guilford Press, 1996).

Vermetten, Eric, and J. Douglas Bremner. "Circuits and Systems in Stress: II. Applications to Neurobiology and Treatment in Posttraumatic Stress Disorder." *Depression and Anxiety* 16, no. 1 (January 2002): pp. 14–38.

Villarreal, Gerardo, Derek A. Hamilton, Helen Petropoulos, Ira Driscoll et al. "Reduced Hippocampal Volume and Total White Matter Volume in Posttraumatic Stress Disorder." *Biological Psychiatry* 52, no. 2 (July 2002): pp. 119–125.

Villarreal, Gerardo, and Cynthia Y. King. "Neuroimaging Studies Reveal Brain Changes in Posttraumatic Stress Disorder." *Psychiatric Annals* 34, no. 11 (November 2004): pp. 845–856.

Vonnegut, Kurt. *Slapstick* (New York: Delacorte Press/Seymour Lawrence, 1976).

————. *Timequake* (New York: G. P. Putnam's Sons, 1997).

Weil, Andrew. *Eating Well for Optimum Health* (New York: Perennial Currents, 2001).

Winnicott, D. W. *The Maturational Processes and the Facilitating Environment: Studies in the Theory of Emotional Development* (London: Karnac Books, 1990).

Winokur, John. *Writers on Writing* (Philadelphia: Running Press, 1990).

Index

About the Author

Karen E. Peterson, Ph.D., a former university writing instructor with an M.A. in English, has served on fiction-writing panels with authors such as Dick Francis; presented workshops for the Key West Literary Seminar, the Rocky Mountain Book Festival, and the National Writers Association; and conducted research on writer's block, procrastination, and Kurt Vonnegut's use of gallows humor. As the author of *The Tomorrow Trap: Unlocking the Secrets of the Procrastination-Protection Syndrome*, she has been featured in the *Boston Globe* and on *CBS This Morning*. As a licensed psychologist and public speaker based in Phoenix, Arizona, she specializes in the treatment of writer's block, procrastination, and AD/HD. She is currently working on two novels, and she is certainly trying not to procrastinate!